riding
the
dragon

SPIRITUAL AND PERSONAL GROWTH BOOKS

BY ROBERT J. WICKS

ROBERT J. WICKS

riding
the
dragon

10 lessons for
inner strength
in
challenging
times

"compassionate and wise"–Jack Kornfield

 SORIN BOOKS   Notre Dame, Indiana

www.sorinbooks.com

International Standard Book Number: 1-893732-65-7

Cover design by Don Nelson

Text design by Katherine Robinson Coleman

Printed and bound in the United States of America.

Library of Congress Cataloging-in-Publication Data

Wicks, Robert J.

  Riding the dragon : 10 lessons for inner strength in challenging times
/ Robert J. Wicks.

    p. cm.

Includes bibliographical references.

  ISBN 1-893732-65-7

  1. Spiritual life. 2. Conduct of life. I. Title.

  BL624.W515 2003

  291.4'4--dc21

                                         2003007149

She welcomes each day with enthusiasm,

laughter, curiosity, and boundless love

for everyone she meets—

I am completely bowled over

by her spirit of spontaneous joy.

For my granddaughter,

Kaitlyn Marie Kulick

Contents

Acknowledgments

I AM GRATEFUL FOR THE WONDERFUL, GENTLE, AND HOPEFUL stories shared with me by Carol Barry, Veronica Cavanaugh-Kennedy, Lucille Winston, Luise Ahrens, and Cindy Boland. Stories like yours help me and others to find, deepen, and share ours. Thank you.

THE HELP KARYN FELDER OFFERED ME WHILE TYPING AND retyping version after version of this book with care and quiet enthusiasm kept me on track. This little book was in process for almost two years, so her patience and attention to detail made all the difference.

FINALLY, FOR HER DEEP, HONEST, AND LOVING REVIEW OF THIS and all of my previous books, I can't put into words my appreciation to my wife Michaele. When I have had the faith and courage to ride the dragons in my life, she had to take much of the heat in order to help me back on when I fell off. Thank you and I love you.

THESE DAYS . . . WE ARE APT TO SEEK OUT A therapist to . . . help us get the dragon back into its cave. Therapists of many schools will oblige in this, and we will thus be returned to what Freud called "ordinary unhappiness," and temporarily, heave a sigh of relief, our repressions working smoothly once again. Zen, by contrast, offers dragon-riding lessons.

DAVID BRAZIER IN *ZEN THERAPY*

WE SHOULD NOT JUST BE A FAN OF DRAGONS; we should always be the dragon himself. Then we will not be afraid of any dragon.[1]

SHUNRYU SUZUKI

introduction

Every problem has two handles.
You can grab it by the handle of fear or
the handle of hope.[2]

MARGARET MITCHELL

A young woman who was studying to be a counselor volunteered some of her free time to sing and play the organ for funerals at her church. During one such occasion, a small, slender little boy came upstairs to the music loft to see her after the service. For him to come upstairs alone was a little odd since children usually don't wander around at a funeral. She asked him if he knew where his parents were. He told her in a very matter-of-fact way, "Well, my mommy is downstairs and she said I could come up to see you. But my daddy is over there" (pointing to the casket downstairs).

Unbeknownst to her, the boy was the son of the man who had just died. She caught her breath and willed herself not to cry, since she was sure this boy had seen enough tears already. She could not help but wonder to herself, though, what in the world was his mother thinking to send him up here? Trying to smile, she looked at him and said, "Oh."

As a counseling student she thought there must be something better to say to a seven-year-old boy who had just lost his father. As it turned out, that one word was sufficient. It reassured him and gave him enough confidence to then tell her, "That song about eagle's wings was my daddy's favorite song; he sung it real loud in church. Now, it's my favorite song too." In response, she nodded her head, smiled, and didn't say another word for fear of crying.

The young boy then went over to the balcony rail and looked down at the casket with the beautiful white lace cover over it sitting in the aisle. He turned around, looked at the young woman, touched the organ keys very quickly, and ran down the stairs. As he left, she tried to say goodbye, but he was gone before she could get the words out.

Several minutes later the widow came upstairs apologizing for her son's intrusion. The young woman reassured her that it was no problem. The boy's mother proceeded to tell her that her son had not spoken one word, cried, or eaten solid food since his dad had died. And then she thanked her for playing "On Eagle's Wings" because it had opened him up.

His name, as she learned later, was Davie—David, Jr.—after his dad. And all she would ever know about him was that his favorite song was "On Eagle's Wings." Yet, she didn't need to know more. The experience itself was enough. It had nurtured her, and she had helped this sad little boy to open up a bit so he could begin to grieve and start to let go.

Of course life doesn't always turn out this way. Poignant healing interactions are rare. Instead, the air seems polluted with negative events, troubled people, and endless demands that quietly drag us down, until we finally hit bottom without realizing how we got there.

Several years ago I remember returning home after a day of seeing patients in my private practice. When I came in, my wife Michaele asked me how my day was. I was ready to say the usual, almost automatic, "fine." But I was overcome with such a deep sense of sadness that I said, "terrible."

"Why, what happened?" she asked. "Did someone say something or do something to ruin your day?"

"No," I replied.

"Then, what makes you say your day was terrible?"

"Because as I went to answer you, I realized I just felt like crying."

Looking at her, I sat down on a kitchen chair without taking off my raincoat. Then as I have taught others, I reviewed the day to see what had happened, what I had blown out of proportion, what erroneous negative belief I was allowing to engulf me.

And then I recognized what it was. It wasn't one specific thing; it was a series of almost unrecognized ones. It wasn't some great problem I had to deal with that day. Instead, as I sat there reflecting, I began to see that over the past few weeks, without realizing it, I had begun to absorb people's anxieties, sadness, helplessness, and hopelessness until I could no longer continue to help them. I had taken in all the abuse, loneliness, financial and marital difficulties, sexual addictions, interpersonal rebuffs, angers, and hardships, and I felt slowly defeated by them. I could now fully appreciate what a student once shared with me in a reflection paper, "I am amazed that so much sadness can fit into my body."

I think that no matter how intelligent we are or how well we take care of ourselves, both acute and chronic stress will occasionally occur. I have learned in my work, though, that the trauma, pressures, busyness, and darkness around us are not the only problems. The real difficulty arises when we don't sit down regularly to take the measure of our lives—whether the times be good or difficult. Paradoxically, difficult times can offer graced moments in a more striking way than the good times can. Through reflection, they can bring us back to the recognition that we can't avoid all trauma or stress. Moreover, we are called neither to win nor to abandon the fight to be a sensitive, joyful, compassionate person, but we are called to live fully. Yet, we also must appreciate that we can only rid the world of darkness through those ways available to us.

Often we seek security by either running away from our feelings of discouragement or attempting to conquer them. Instead, we need to stay with them; in Jungian terms, we need to make friends with our shadow. The Zen masters have another way of saying this: we need to learn to "ride the dragon." How we can do this is a subject that I will develop in this brief book.

We need to see how we have relied too much on ourselves, and that in focusing on the problems of the world, we have often forgotten to see what is beautiful and right in it. In an interview in the magazine *Common Boundary* a number of years ago, the Zen roshi (teacher) Thich Nhat Hanh said, "During the [Vietnam] war, we were so busy helping the wounded that we sometimes forgot to smell the flowers. Night has a very pleasant smell [here], especially in the country. But we would forget to pay attention to the smell of mint, coriander, thyme, and sage."

We could see this awareness in the hopeful attitude of those professionals who helped out after the September 11 terrorist attack. They had seen the cruelty and devastation, but they also saw the goodness in all those working together on the scene.

Sitting down with our own life in a gentle, clear-headed way can remind us of the beauty right before us. Reflection and small, significant actions based on what we learn each day about ourselves and life can't eliminate the natural stresses of life or its pain; however, a well-spent time-out can help us to prevent unnecessary suffering, to learn from the pain we shouldn't avoid, and to pay attention to the "mint, coriander, thyme, and sage" that are the fragrances of our lives, no matter what the circumstances. Fully appreciating our journey as we are living it—not seeking or settling for elusive future fantasies or becoming mired down in mere nostalgia—is what really matters.

Balancing compassion for others with a deep kindness and reverence for our own inner self can actually be quite simple and powerful if we take the time to do it right. To do this we need the psychological and spiritual tools with which to work, what author Margaret Mitchell calls "the handle of hope." I have learned this time and again from reflecting on my own life and the unusual and rewarding work I do with others.

My clients are very challenging people— professional helpers and healers. When physicians, nurses, psychotherapists, ministers, relief workers, or educators become temporarily lost or overwhelmed, I walk with them. When the intensity of their efforts to help others causes them to experience confusion, turmoil, darkness, distress, or trauma, I work to help them make sense of it all.

Since these clients are engaged in the healing professions themselves, they don't allow me much margin for error. They want and expect effective, brief, powerful interventions for their burnout and/or loss of perspective. While working with this unique population, I have come to understand that not only are these helpers learning comforting, hard-won wisdom, they are also teaching me important ways to open new doors of psychological liberation and inner spiritual rejuvenation.

If we are willing to spend a little time each day reflecting on our lives and learning these simple truths, we will benefit from the wisdom of self-care. With brief powerful interventions we can quickly chart a clearer course each day to uncover healing psychological and spiritual truths—no matter how stressful the day might be. Given all we have experienced recently, if ever a resource were needed, it is now.

Although I found that reflecting on proven insights from my own clinical practice was a valuable resource, the insights alone were not sufficient. More important is being faithful to the wisdom I have gleaned from an array of spiritual traditions on how to discover and strengthen our inner selves. I need to be aware of and faithful to both the spiritual and psychological in order to live fully myself as I support the others who come to me as well.

Essential Psychological and Spiritual Wisdom

Early in his wonderful book *After the Ecstasy, the Laundry*, American Buddhist teacher Jack Kornfield warns about the care we should take in embarking on a true inner journey. Most people, if asked, say they want to live a rich spiritual and psychologically aware life. However, making such a commitment, while laudable and understandable, is more serious and has greater consequences than many realize. It is not an easy commitment to undertake and remain faithful to in today's world. Kornfield illustrates this:

> When the Tibetan teacher Chogyam Trungpa arrived late, as usual, to a crowded San Francisco lecture hall, he offered a refund to anyone who did not want to stay. He warned those who were new that a true spiritual path is arduous and demanding, involving "one insult after another." So he suggested that those with doubts not embark. "If you haven't started, it's best not to begin." Then he looked steadily around the room and said, "But if you have begun, *it is best to finish*." (emphasis added)

Once again, to finish the journey today, fathoming both psychological and spiritual wisdom is imperative.

With an appreciation of this, in the spring of 1988 I wrote to the well-known spiritual guide and author Henri Nouwen. I wanted to offer him some encouragement at a time of great inner crisis in his own life. At the same time I wanted to bring him up-to-date on the next book I was planning to write and ask if he thought there was any merit in it. The theme of the book addressed the psychological perils of spiritual intimacy. My feeling was that this might strike a chord with him, especially at what was a tender juncture in his own life. As it turned out, I was right because he wrote the following gracious response:

Dear Bob:

Thanks so much for your good letter. I really appreciate your staying in touch and your support during this time of my life. I have still not returned to Daybreak and it might take me a few more months before I am able to do so, but I am gradually discovering some new inner strength and I hope very much that I will be able to continue my ministry with the L'Arche community before too long.

It means a lot to me that you keep in touch and that you are willing to support me with your prayers. If anything holds me up, it is the prayers of friends and I rely on them. What I am experiencing is a really deep spiritual crisis in which I realize that God wants all of my heart, not simply a part of it. It seems as if He wants to test my faithfulness and my commitment in a new way. He is really asking me to let go of everything that does not bring me closer to Him. He calls me to a more generous prayer life and to a more fearless ministry. This year is a kind of desert year to purify my heart. It is painful, but also full of grace.

Meanwhile, I hope that your summer will be good and creative, and, most of all, prayerful. I am very interested in your new book. I am even curious to know which psychological perils you have in mind. I am so used to reading about the spiritual perils of psychological intimacy, that I am very curious to know more about the psychological perils of spiritual intimacy. Enclosed I send you a little book just published, as a sign of my friendship and love.

With warm greetings,

Yours,
Henri

Although Henri's interest and curiosity concerning my approach should have been enough to nudge me to proceed, for various reasons I set the idea aside. Then, a decade later, an event in my life made me return to and deepen the project. It was an unexpected dark journey of my own which confused and overwhelmed me. It was also the added impetus to structure the core of the spiritual and psychological wisdom I had used, and to integrate spiritual wisdom from the east and west. After all, the person in peril now was me.

Into the Basement

My slide into darkness was surprisingly swift. I was in a free fall. As I sat at my lowest point, I realized I was experiencing a "reverse spiritual transfusion." Slowly, I could feel the energy, the hope, and my consciousness of belief in myself fading.

It all began with problems at work. Where once my efforts were viewed as creative and visionary, they were now seen by a key administrator as erratic. Where once I had been given freedom and trust, now new structure and checks and balances were imposed.

My first response was to fight. Then slowly I felt defeated and began to let go and descend into the basement of my soul. Psychologically I started to feel what it really meant to be in one's shadow. Being an optimistic person at heart I also thought, "As long as I am down here in the spiritual basement, I might as well look around." And I did.

I began to realize that while I didn't agree with the style and methods of the person who triggered the slide, this was not really about him. It was about me and my idols. I realized I had forgotten about faithfulness and replaced it with a shallow desire for success.

I no longer appreciated the real joy of achievement and instead involved myself in competition. I learned a great deal while in my basement. The self-knowledge even made me feel somewhat exhilarated, and I shared this with a colleague who is a very experienced Jungian analyst. I told him, "Entering into my shadow was very helpful for me, Bill. I saw a great deal about myself, but I would never have gone down into my spiritual basement to see what was stored there if it were left to me." To this he smiled and responded softly, "No one willingly goes into their own shadow, Bob. They are pushed! But at least you've chosen to learn from the experience and that is wonderful."

Following this, metaphorically I climbed the stairs out of the basement armed with new knowledge to help myself and others. But surprisingly when I tried the door to the first floor, it was locked. I thought I was done, but I wasn't, and as I turned around in my mind's eye, I saw a glimmer coming from the basement. There was yet another place to go.

As I descended with a renewed but greater sense of defeat, I could see there was a spiritual and psychological sub-basement where I must go. As I went down there, for the first time in my life I felt I might never return to a place of perspective and peace.

Softening the Soul

As I sat in this new deeper darkness, I knew I had nowhere to go to escape. It was all night. Slowly, steadily I began to see the hurt I had caused people close to me—family, old friends, new friends, acquaintances, those who had worked for and with me, as well as those I was called upon to assist. It was a very disorienting experience to say the least— especially for someone who worked the past twenty years as a therapist for professional healers and helpers.

"Physician heal thyself" kept echoing in my ears, but I couldn't. The only thing I could do was to stare into the darkness of the truth and let it soften my soul. I knew that when you add humility to knowledge you have an opportunity for wisdom. And, when you let wisdom meet the grace of God, love and freedom in life become possible. But at that point, these were still just nice words.

I felt I could do very little by myself. But what I could do, I knew I must. Hiding was not the answer. I knew I had to stare into the truth of my failures. The Jewish theologian Abraham Joshua Heschel was right when he said, "An act of injustice is condemned, not because the law is broken, but because a person has been hurt." And I started to see all the harm I had caused others in so many ways during my life.

A patient had once given me a poster of a rag doll flattened after being put through a wringer. Under the picture it said, "The truth shall set you free . . . but first it will make you miserable." I felt that way. It was as if every time I tried to get up, another wave of awful realization would hit me about hurt I had caused, and

I would be knocked down again. Just when I would start to see a glimmer of hope, some direction, a way forward, I would be thrown back. Once I even remember sitting quietly and thinking, "Am I really such an awful, hurtful person, and if so, is there, was there never any real good in me? Is there no way out of this terrible experience of darkness?"

In the past, the way out was often running away. I knew it from my work as a therapist as well as from my study of western spirituality, insight psychotherapy, and—more lately—the interface between Zen Buddhism and therapy. As a matter of fact, one well-known Zen therapist felt that though the very act of facing the truth is essential to live a compassionate and wise life, even most of us who are helpers and healers shy away from it in our work with others. In the words of David Brazier from his brilliant work *Zen Therapy*:

> These days . . . we are apt to seek out a therapist to . . . help us get the dragon back into its cave. Therapists of many schools will oblige in this, and we will thus be returned to what Freud called "ordinary unhappiness," and, temporarily, heave a sigh of relief, our repressions working smoothly once again. Zen, by contrast, offers *dragon-riding lessons.* (emphasis added)

Such dragon-riding lessons, I believed, would not only open me to receive the grace of new light, but as weak as I felt, somehow I believed that eventually these new truths, if faced, would enable me in some mysterious way to be a better person for others. The words from Rainer Maria Rilke's classic *Letters to a Young Poet* came back to me once again:

> Do not believe that he who seeks to comfort you lives untroubled among the simple and quiet words that sometimes do you good. His life has much difficulty and sadness and remains far behind yours. Were it otherwise he would never have been able to find those words.

What would I use to guide myself and others who found themselves in darkness and wanted to take advantage of the darkness they were in? Would it be all I had learned about self-care from my work with professional helpers and healers? Would it be the themes presented by spiritual guides like Henri Nouwen, Thomas Merton, Abraham Heschel, or the desert *ammas* and *abbas* of the fourth and fifth centuries whose wisdom is still filled with clarity and challenge today?

Or would I draw from the wonderful western writers such as David Brazier, Jack Kornfield, Pema Chödrön, and Andrew Harvey who are interpreting eastern thought, or from a Tibetan Buddhist writer such as Sogyal Rinpoche, all of whom had been so helpful to me of late? Now I felt the need more than ever before to integrate and structure all of them in the most simple, accessible way possible for use by myself and others. The result of these efforts is *Riding the Dragon*.

A Journey With Direction

I feel deeply that I, those who come to see me, and you are motivated to grow and deepen ourselves. The story John F. Kennedy used to tell about one of his favorite authors seems to fit the challenge we have set out before us:

> Frank O'Connor, the Irish author, tells in one of his books how as a boy, he and his friends would make their way across the countryside and when they came to an orchard wall that seemed too high and too doubtful to try, and too difficult to permit their voyage to continue, they would take off their hats and toss them over the wall—and then they had no choice but to follow them![3]

The lessons that follow are designed to offer some sense of direction to help us go after the hats we have already thrown over the wall in our commitment to a life of wisdom, peace, and compassion. Even in the darkness there are many gifts present if we have the courage, faithfulness, and humility to see them. As David Brazier pointed out, the temptation is to push the dragon of truth back into the cave. If you wish to do this and still can, stop now and you'll still probably have a life filled with nice experiences. But, if you want to join yourself with the wisdom available to teach us how to live as much of life as fully as we can in the short time we are here, then "riding the dragon" is the only path worth taking.

Like the young organist's experience with the grieving little boy, all of us have known the significant impact that offering a comforting word or two can have on others. Similarly, this book is designed to offer comforting—and sometimes appropriately challenging—words to ourselves. In doing so, the positive long-lasting results that are possible will not only aid us to be the calm in a storm, but will also help us to enjoy our whole lives more fully. Moreover, we can also—in the process—have a healing impact on those with whom we interact, and this is no small gift in a world presently experiencing such dark times.

enhancing your use of the lessons

most people have developed their own unique way of incorporating what they read into their daily lives. However, to enhance your use of the lessons that follow, some other approaches you may wish to consider are:

- ~ Read daily with an open heart
- ~ Carry the quotes and stories within
- ~ Overlearn the lessons
- ~ Form a nest with meditation
- ~ Mix with daily life
- ~ Discuss with spiritual friends for the journey
- ~ Persevere in faith when doubt and failure occur

Read Daily With an Open Heart

The best advice I can give you about the learning and living out of these lessons is not to underestimate their power because of their surprising simplicity. If we read, reflect on, and listen with an open heart to the brief lessons condensed in this book for a short time each day—day after day—the seeds of perspective, passion, and hope should establish themselves and grow strong. This in turn will help shrink many of the negative preoccupations and habits that interfere with personal growth. In doing this, they can also provide basic perspective and peace, serve to nurture a hopeful heart, and encourage a spirit of intrigue and passion about our lives that can be quite exhilarating—even when times are stressful and confusing.

Carry the Quotes and Stories Within

Winston Churchill once said, "It is a good thing to read books of quotations. The qualities, when engraved upon the memory, give you good thoughts." The quotes and stories in this book are not intended to be entertaining throwaways but are meant to be carried with you—within. They help us to see things differently. Most times that's all it takes to make big changes. Even if you don't have the time to read a chapter, the quotes and stories take only seconds. Then by recalling them during the day, you can quickly bring the lesson to mind.

Overlearn the Lessons

Each chapter will hold a lesson for you—probably a unique one in your case. Overlearning it helps it not to fade. To overlearn, I write out a one-line lesson and review it again and again—even using it in conversation.

Form a Nest With Meditation

After reading quotes, stories, and lessons, let them seed the unconscious by following them with daily meditation, perhaps in the morning. Don't use lack of time as a defense. If you don't have twenty minutes, then take two. You can always be two minutes late, and this minimum will help you get into a regular rhythm of centering yourself quietly before becoming busy.

Mix With Daily Life

Look for opportunities to mix your quotes, stories, lessons, and meditations with daily life. Otherwise, what you've learned may not endure in the way you'd like. Practice the lessons you value with family, friends, coworkers, and strangers. Act as if they exist already as part of your style.

Discuss With Spiritual Friends for the Journey

Develop a circle of friends who are also interested in the inner journey and discuss your impressions of the material in the book. It will help you stay on course. Good friends keep us faithful—that is why *zazen* (sitting meditation) is best done in groups. Also, different voices will help you avoid getting off on a tangent or over/underemphasizing some particular insight. Encouraging, teasing, prophetic, and serious voices should all be a part of your circle.

Persevere in Faith When Doubt and Failure Occur

Doubt and failure are part of every serious inner journey. The Koran counsels, "God helps those who persevere." Jesus says, "If you have faith the size of a mustard seed . . . nothing will be impossible for you" (Mt 17:20). As we shall see in the pages to come, overcoming doubt and failure is not at issue. Learning from them is. Both are tools used to see where our inner challenges lie and to remember that humility is one of the major cornerstones of the spiritual life. With such a virtue, we will be open and flexible at every turn of our life.

A Final Comment

If any of the above ideas interfere or weigh down the way you flow with the lessons in this book, drop them. Trust your own intuition on what works best for you. Like the lessons to follow, they are meant only to enhance the style of learning and living you already have.

Lesson 1

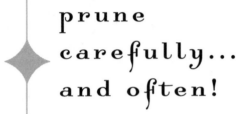

p r u n e
c a r e f u l l y . . .
a n d o f t e n !

We need only look at all the people who rushed to help after the September 11 terrorist attacks in the United States to see the value of pruning. When needs are perceived, action is prized—no matter what the personal consequences are.

Contrary to popular thinking, I don't believe most people are self-centered today. In fact, in my experience, the opposite is true.

One of the greatest gifts we can offer when we reach out to those who need help—family members, coworkers, friends, and those we meet each day—is a sense of our own peace. Paradoxically, a serious obstacle to doing this is failing to take responsibility for properly focusing and limiting our giving, lest our reaching out to others becomes undisciplined activism prompted by anxiety, duty, and guilt (what I call superego compassion) rather than by a true attitude of kindness (ego compassion).

In 1985 I visited with Henri Nouwen, while he was teaching at Harvard University, to reflect on my work and life. As we sat in his kitchen we discussed the early chapters of a manuscript I was writing on the topic of availability. Being a very practical person—as well as inspired—Nouwen emphasized not only the gift of availability but also its dangers. In the midst of one of his sentences, he stopped and said, "There must be a scriptural theme that makes the point I wish to emphasize." Then, his face lit up and he said, "Pruning! That's it. Pruning is the theme I was looking for. It not only speaks of cutting back but also of the ultimate blossoming that takes place when it is done properly."

This theme has remained with me as I have moved through my life and work. It is rewarding to prune our inner life of the causes and tendencies that block true discernment of what burdens we should and should not carry. And in the end it will reward those we are called to help. Moreover, becoming aware of and sensitive to the unrealistic expectations others have requires that we recognize how easily our natural efforts to be helpful can become distorted.

In my travels I heard a story about a priest who spent part of each night making sandwiches for the homeless. He would travel around the poorer parts of the city and distribute them. Even though his day was already full, this late night activity didn't overwhelm him. It actually made him happy. He didn't do it out of guilt, duty, or external pressure. He shared freely and openly in a way that made a difference for him. Even when the street people rebuffed his offer of food, he didn't feel rejected or angry, because he wasn't doing it for the reward of acceptance or appreciation.

The media found out about him and printed a story about his work. Instantly his reputation grew and he became a minor celebrity. The public, even his fellow priests, started sending him money to support his ministry. Much to their surprise he sent back the money to everyone with a one-line note that said: "Make your own damn sandwiches!"

This man obviously knew who he was. He didn't let the needs, expectations, and projections of others infect his own simple sense of mission in life. He wasn't manipulated by the reactions—even flattery—of others, as many of us are. His sense of personal satisfaction wasn't dependent primarily on the approval of others. Everyone enjoys being liked and admired. It's natural to enjoy positive responses from others. The question this man had obviously asked himself and responded to appropriately is one we need to pose to ourselves: When does the cost of approval become too psychologically and spiritually expensive? The reality we must face is that what we do for others is often not enough to satisfy them. Given the great needs of many of the people who surround us, no one person can do everything, no matter how loving he or she may be.

Have you ever felt that the more you seem to do for others, the more dissatisfied some of them are? Or the more you try to be a good parent, daughter, physician, friend, or helper, the more guilty you feel? Silly, isn't it? Yet those are negative reactions we experience when we haven't taken time to become centered, to understand and reflect on what our mission is—what we're called to be in life. Not having a sense of what we should do and be in life makes us prey to the undue influence and control of others. Rather than exercising our desire to do something good, regardless of the results, we become manipulated by guilt, the reactions of others, and a distorted sense of duty. Sadly, little peace is experienced by either the giver or receiver when this happens. Moreover, at the critical moment when people really do need us to walk the extra mile with them, we pull back because we are just too tired to go on.

In many currently popular books, a solution to personal exhaustion and feeling overextended is to simplify your life, which is a good place to start. However, in addition to trimming the externals of our lives so we can live in a manageable way, an even more important inner simplification or pruning must take place. In therapy, mentoring, and spiritual guidance, people are taught to practice an inner pruning process. They are taught to "take a psychological and spiritual step back" when beginning to feel overwhelmed. One way to do this is to search the motives, fears, expectations, and habits that are causing our discomfort.

Taking this step back is not easy. If we pull back for reassessment, we may worry about other people's reactions or fear possible rejection. We may not want to look at our own motivations for fear of finding them selfish. Yet, when we do take the time and space to quietly and gently question ourselves, we can get clear on what is happening, and take steps to correct it.

Availability to others relies directly on our ability to prune poor motivations so we are not prey to unrealistic expectations—either ours or those of others. When we do this the natural beauty of our life will spontaneously emerge and nurture others.

Several years ago there was a show on Irish television called *The Gay Byrne Hour.* Some loved it, some hated it, but almost everyone watched it. One of the special features of the show was a live Christmas Eve broadcast held outside on Grafton Street, a main street running through Dublin. During this particular show the host would invite people to spontaneously sing, tell stories, and interact with him.

One Christmas, a young woman convinced a friend to go with her to Grafton Street and try to get on the show. She had a good voice and thought it would be fun to test her talent in a live broadcast, never expecting the chance would actually present itself.

She and her friend went, and much to her surprise and delight, she was picked out of the crowd and asked if she would be interested in telling a story or singing something. She said she would be happy to share a song and started singing "O Holy Night." People who were present said that as she was singing, all of Grafton Street gradually went silent. She sang like an angel. A man living in Ireland at the time told me that he felt almost all of Ireland went silent. One voice. No expectations from within herself or others. It was the unexpected hand of wonder in the ordinary. Never could this woman have expected the impact she would have. Yet, as in the case of the priest who made sandwiches for the homeless, it was a natural way for her to share herself. The process of giving was the reward.

If only we could remember to prune away the unrealistic expectations, then the simple gifts we have could be shared without so much stress. They could reap rewards in sometimes unseen ways, no matter what the apparent results seem to be. But it is not easy to withstand the influence of a world so bent on overt accomplishments and public achievements. Still, when we are able to set aside the need for ongoing successes and ceaseless praise, not only will we feel a sense of joy, but we will touch many others with that same joy as well.

There is a cemetery in the United States famous for its impressive monuments. Probably the most imposing among them is one for a deceased military hero—a general. It lists all of the battles he fought and his lifetime accomplishments. Right next to it is a small stone erected for a beloved young wife who died when she was only twenty-one years old. Unlike the general's long epitaph, her grieving husband had only one line engraved in remembrance of her:

Everywhere she went,
she brought flowers.

As Nouwen pointed out, the blossoms are the ultimate benefit of pruning. When we do this inner pruning, we are more likely to be aware of the flowers we bring to those we encounter along the way. Knowing this helps us to step back and reassess when we feel overwhelmed by unrealistic expectations that we or others hold. This first lesson on pruning relies on our ability to gain such a sense of perspective by ensuring we are clear about our goals, especially when we are exerting more and more effort and feeling less and less satisfied by what we are doing. It is stepping back and reflecting on our motivations that makes all the difference.

Lesson 2

recognize
your
renewal zones

When speaking with helping professionals after the September 11 attack on the U.S., I saw the feelings of futility in their faces. This was not surprising. I had seen such looks before during my two visits to Cambodia to work with employees of social service organizations working there. I saw how drained they were by their efforts to reach out to the Khmer people who were suffering from years of torture and horror. Some workers had never taken off two days in a row because they felt guilty that they were not doing enough.

I saw it again in the faces of relief workers evacuated to the U.S. from Rwanda and Angola after atrocities and violence pulled those countries apart. Like most survivors of catastrophes, they viewed their situation with a feeling of luck and guilt for having been spared, for being able to move on.

As I listened to their stories of guilt, frustration, and futility in such situations, often I felt myself pulled in the same downward direction. I started to think: "What can I do? I'm just listening. What good is that?" As soon as I became aware of this negative mood change, I stepped back within myself and realized how important the gift of a listening presence is. I also became thankful that I have carefully taken care of myself. By availing myself of the safe zones in my life, I can stay afloat to both relish and share my life with others who are undergoing rough times. After all, what good can you be to others if you've let yourself burn out in the process?

Sometimes the stress we face at work mingles with what we must face in our personal lives, and if we are not careful, we can sink psychologically and spiritually. Once, after a very intense couple of weeks in my own life, I decided to deal with the stress by stepping back slightly from my normal routine. Though usually an early riser, I rescheduled my early appointments and planned to sleep in a bit later the coming morning.

Instead, a ringing phone woke me even earlier than normal. Still half asleep I couldn't figure out what the caller was trying to tell me and I said so. She finally realized she had woken me up and started her story again:

"There was a tornado yesterday here in Maryland and it killed two college students who were sisters, and injured their father."

"I'm not sure why you're calling me about this?"

"Well, the young women were daughters of a woman with whom your wife taught."

That's how the day—and next few weeks—got started.

When I arrived at the college later that morning, there was an e-mail from someone at the Pentagon regarding the impact that the terrorist attack continued to have on his coworkers. This was quickly followed by a visit from someone who debriefed White House staffers following threats to their safety.

As I sat with all of this, the phone rang. It was my wife calling to tell me that her sister, who was at the heart of the family, had died in New York City. In several hours we would be on the road.

My first thought after this quick succession of events was: "Let me go home before anything else happens!" After arranging for the necessary coverage while I would be away, I went down to my car only to find a student sitting stunned and crying in the car next to mine. She was from New Zealand and had just received word that her father was dying. Shocked and upset, she was uncertain about whether or not she should make the twenty-hour flight home now or wait.

After we reflected about this for a few minutes, I offered a few words of support and went home. There I found out that traveling to New York would not be easy. Officers of the Bridge and Tunnel Authority were stopping automobiles and doing random checks because of a bomb threat. Consequently, traffic entering the city was backed up for hours. So, we took the train.

During my sister-in-law's wake, I spoke with family members who were involved in the rescue and security details at the World Trade Center. Their stories were poignant, powerful, and moving, but I didn't realize how deeply those stories affected me until one of my nephews, Larry Lanza, began to speak about the search dogs:

"Then there was the problem with the dogs, Uncle Bob."

"What problem?"

"When they couldn't find anyone alive, they became depressed, wouldn't even drink water, and had to be evacuated to an area away from the scene where we could replenish their fluids intravenously."

"Where did you evacuate them to?" was my response.

To be honest, I really didn't care where they were evacuated to. However, I could feel myself sliding spiritually and psychologically into my own darkness. I reacted by asking a cognitive question to *catch the slide* (the subject of the next chapter) in order to avoid becoming overfilled and overwhelmed emotionally while listening to these sad stories.

The next weekend, after returning from the funeral, I received a call from Toronto. The caller introduced herself as the head of a large school board and went on to say: "Our keynote speaker's brother just died." My first thought was to ask "What has this to do with me?" but instead I simply said, "I'm not sure why you are telling me?"

"Well, we'd like you to fly up tomorrow and take her place giving the keynote to 10,000 educators in the Air Canada Arena." So, I flew to Toronto.

A week later I was in Oklahoma to give a two-day workshop. As soon as I arrived, those organizing the event brought me to the now famous site in Oklahoma City, the memorial to the 1995 bombing of the Murrah Federal Building.

The memorial features a collection of individual clear Lucite chairs, and as I stood there looking numbly at them—one for each person who had died—I noticed some were smaller and asked why they were different. The woman with me explained that these were for the children who had died. And, as we walked closer to them, I saw that grieving relatives had put stuffed animals on some of them. I could feel the slide again.

Sometimes—especially on days like that—an interesting image comes to mind when I think of my own life and those of the professional helpers and healers who come to me for mentoring. It's an image of a person standing in a pool facing the deep end with the water level just below his nose. As he stands there, he sees a line of people ready to cannonball off the diving board in order to inundate him where he stands.

We all have to deal with real crises and daily stresses. We may not be the firemen cleaning up at the World Trade Center, finding human arms and heads, discovering a fellow fireman only recognizable by the uniform he is wearing. But all of us are somehow affected by life's traumatic events.

In addition to this reality, the out of the ordinary pressures we have at work don't allow us to put our personal pressures on hold. For example, when I was experiencing the surprising demands I just described, I was still responsible for my job at the college and for my role in the family. Such responsibilities do not disappear in times of crisis.

When the Catholic Archdiocese of Boston called me in 2002 to help their priests stay afloat during the pedophilia crisis, which was demoralizing innocent, hard working priests, I reminded them of this:

> You are under a great deal of stress and suspicion now even though you are innocent. As Cardinal O'Connor said back in 1993 when New York was facing a similar crisis, "It's getting increasingly difficult for some priests and some bishops to hold their heads up. Everyone

is under suspicion . . . a grenade could explode at any time, and another and another."

However, the stress does not end there for you. Many of you have sick or dying parents whom you must visit and care for. And, even if you are spared this, you still must meet the overwhelming demands of guiding a parish during times when the challenges are more complicated and staffing is so poor because of the shortage of priests.

Add all of this up and you have a psychologically dangerous and spiritually-depleting situation if you don't take the time and care to renew and develop new awareness to strengthen your inner self.

Along with the big things, we must also deal with the ocean of little annoyances in life. There are people, for instance, who call or write with petty problems and complaints that probably make us wonder "Where do you get the time to be such a pain in the rear end? Don't you have anything else to do?" The truly unavoidable stresses can combine with the irritating complaints to swamp and overwhelm us— especially if we don't have renewal zones to protect us. Renewal zones provide us with a respite, a place for inner refreshment and reappraisal, and a chance to have some good old-fashioned fun.

When adults feel safe, relax, and have fun with family or friends, therapists refer to it as "regression in the service of the ego." The absence of the chance to be a kid again, to be free and spontaneous, to laugh, joke, and tease people is psychologically dangerous.

When we have to watch every word, when we have to walk on eggshells, when we have no relationships in which to be ourselves, then burnout is sure to follow. And so we need personal renewal zones where we have space to be free, to be ordinary, to be ourselves. If we don't have such spaces, we not only experience distress but also the possibility of compassion fatigue, anomie, alcohol/drug abuse, or physical illness. It can even lead to an unnecessary job change, divorce, or a psychological disorder.

The self is limited. It has only so much energy. If it is not renewed, then depletion will take place. Too often we don't avail ourselves of the type of activities that truly renew us. When this occurs we run a greater risk that we will unnecessarily lose perspective and burn out, which is not only sad for us but for the people we are in a position to help in our circle of family, friends, and coworkers. Then, sometime when we least expect it, something happens to wake us up to how foolish we've been. In my own case, I still remember when this happened to me . . . a story that I first related in my book *After Fifty*:

> A number of years ago a very close friend of mine in his early forties was dying from brain cancer. He was outrageous and we constantly teased one another. Even though he was dying, this did not stop.

He had been living in New York and I hadn't seen much of him in the years since I was the best man at his wedding. When he was hospital- ized in Philadelphia to undergo experimental treatment, I visited him. When I came to visit he had already been there for almost two weeks.

When I inquired about his health he shared a summary of his condition, which included loss of short-term memory. So, I said to him: "You mean you can't even remember what happened yesterday?" He said: "No."

"So," I said, "if I were here yesterday you wouldn't remember my visit?" He said: "No."

Then I smiled and said: "So, you don't remem- ber me coming in and sitting here with you each day for five hours for the past two weeks?" He looked at me, hesitated for a second or two, grinned widely, and said . . . well, I can't share exactly what he said—after all, this is a spiritu- al book—but together we both had a good laugh over it.

One of the things he did surprise me with, though, was a question that really helped me put my activities in perspective. He asked: "What good things are you doing now?" As I started to launch into an obsessive (naturally well-organized) list of my recent academic and professional accomplishments, he interrupted me by saying: "No, not that stuff. I mean what really good things have you done? When have you gone fishing last? What museums have you visited lately? What good movies have you seen in the past month?"

The "good things" he was speaking about the last time I saw him alive were different from the ones I in my arrogant good health thought about. Unfortunately, I have a lot of company in this regard.

See and Enjoy the Spiritual and Psychological Oases Life Provides

Camels are fascinating animals. They can walk through the desert carrying their cargo for days without water. They are able to carry very heavy burdens. Yet, even these wonderfully sturdy animals will dry up, fall down, and die if they are unable to find water and rest at some point. Even the strongest among us must stop for renewal in the oases that dot the parched deserts of life.

Like sturdy camels, healing professionals are able to journey with others in the most difficult circumstances, helping them shoulder their burdens through psychological and spiritual deserts without frequent nourishment for themselves.

I have found this metaphor to be a good guide for the professional helpers and healers who come to me for therapy and mentoring. I have used it personally to avoid losing my way amidst the stresses and developmental challenges of life.

In working with people in crisis, physicians, nurses, educators, psychotherapists, relief workers, and people in full-time ministry walk a tightrope between callousness and over-involvement. As one minister put it when he was asked what his role was with those he served: "I walk with people through the night."

For helpers and healers to survive and thrive amidst such professional and personal stress, trauma, and uncertainty, they must find oases of peace and joy or they will dry up themselves. As the psychotherapist in Lawrence Sanders' novel *The Case of Lucy Bending* stated,

> Most laymen, he supposed, believed psychiatrists fell apart under the weight of other people's problems. Dr. Theodore Levin had another theory. He feared that a psychiatrist's life force gradually leaked out. It was expended on sympathy, understanding, and the obsessive need to heal and help create whole lives. Other people's lives. But always from the outside. Always the observer. Then one day he would wake up and discover that he himself was empty, drained.

So, what is the answer to this? Obviously there isn't one simple response available to keep compassionate persons afloat in difficult times. However, a primary and effective response is to be aware of our own safe zones and oases. Then we need to visit them on a regular basis in order to avoid drowning in the stress that comes our way.

And so, when people feel under great stress both at home and at work, I suggest they check to see if they have other renewal zones in their lives, and if not, to implement them quickly. Try the following as renewal zones.

~ Quiet walks by yourself

~ Time and space for meditation

~ Spiritual and recreational reading—including the diaries and biographies of others whom you admire

~ Some light exercise (as approved by your physician)

~ Opportunities to laugh offered by movies, cheerful friends, etc.

~ A hobby such as gardening

~ Phone calls to family and friends who inspire and tease you

~ Involvement in projects that renew

~ Listening to music you enjoy

It really doesn't take much for me to regain perspective and become refreshed, if I take out a little time to be renewed. Listening to music from the Celtic version of the *Secret Garden* eases my soul when I am tense. A short walk in the woods detoxifies my spirit when I'm preoccupied with the sadness, futility, and fear I have encountered.

Renewal zones are essential, then, if we are to remain vital, compassionate, and grateful in life. Often we go too long without checking to see if these interpersonal spaces are present. Unfortunately, we either take such things for granted or see them as luxuries, and before too long we have to deal with consequences that we could have avoided through early intervention. We need to ask ourselves an important question and perhaps even do so on a daily basis: If we don't take primary responsibility for the care of ourselves and model healthy self-renewal for those who respect us, then who do we think will do it? This is especially the case when we face traumatic experiences. And so, we need to be alert to opportunities to drink in the gifts of life so we can meet extraordinary demands when they arise.

If there are places and people with whom we can laugh, relax, dream, and plot the future, then discouragement need not take root or flourish. People who can encourage, challenge, and be fun-loving companions can go a long way in preventing or stemming burnout. Whereas, if all the places in our life—work, home, and recreation—and the people who inhabit them are filled with worry, anxiety, anger, or angst, the interpersonal space we occupy will always be gray. When this is so, compassion fatigue and a sense that life has lost its joy will become evident. Keeping an eye out for the oases in our lives and expanding their presence and use are just common sense. Once again, we should not only do this for ourselves but for those who count on us to be a healing presence in their lives. We can't share what we don't have. It is as simple as that.

Lesson 3

catch
the
slide

nnie Dillard, in her book *The Writing Life,* notes that "in working class France, when an apprentice got hurt or when he got tired, the experienced worker said: 'It is the trade entering his body.'" Similarly, when the daily pressures of our lives seem to tip the scale we too become tired and frustrated; it is the compassionate life entering our body.

A life of caring is never easy and sometimes pushes us into irritation. After a day especially filled with aggravations and ridiculous requests, a pastor sat down to dinner with his hair all askew, said a prayer of thanks, turned to his dinner guest, and said with a sigh, "I get the feeling that early this morning someone put a sign on the door that read: If you're nuts, knock here!"

Sometimes things get much worse than this, though. As we listen to stories of terrible things that happen to a family member or coworker, we catch some of their futility, fear, vulnerability, and hopelessness rather than experiencing mere frustration or concern. We learn that no matter how professionally prepared we are, we are not immune to the psychological and spiritual dangers that arise in living a full life of involvement with others. I remember learning this the hard way myself.

In 1994 I did a psychological debriefing of some of the relief workers evacuated from Rwanda's bloody civil war. I interviewed each person and gave them an opportunity to tell their stories. As they related the horrors they had experienced, they seemed to be grateful for an opportunity to ventilate. They recounted the details again and again, relating their feelings as well as descriptions of the events which triggered them. Their sense of futility, their feelings of guilt, their sense of alienation, their experiences with emotional outbursts, all came to the fore.

In addition to listening, I gave them handouts on what to possibly expect down the road (problems sleeping, difficulties trusting and relating to others, flashbacks and the like). As I moved through the process of debriefing and providing information so they could have a frame of reference for understanding their experiences, I thought to myself, "This is going pretty well." Then, something happened that shifted my whole experience.

In the course of one of the final interviews, one of the relief workers related stories of how certain members of the Hutu tribe raped and dismembered their Tutsi foes. Soon, I noticed I was holding onto my chair for dear life. I was doing what some young people call "white knuckling it."

After the session, I did what I usually do after an intense encounter—a psychospiritual countertransferential review. (If time doesn't permit then, I do it at the end of the day—every day.) In doing this, I get in touch with my feelings by asking myself: What made me sad? Overwhelmed me? Sexually aroused me? Made me extremely happy or even confused me? Being brutally honest with myself, I try to put my finger on the pulse of my emotions.

The first thing that struck me about this particular session was the tight grip I had on the chair as the session with the relief worker progressed. "What was I feeling when I did this? Why did I do this?"

It didn't take me long to realize that their terrible stories had broken through my defenses and temporarily destroyed my normal sense of distance and detachment. I was holding onto the chair because, quite simply, I was frightened to death that if I didn't, I would be pulled into the vortex of darkness myself.

That recognition alone helped lessen the pain and my fearful uneasiness. I then proceeded with a combination of a countertransferential review and theological reflection. These are tools used by therapists and ministers to prevent the slide into unnecessary darkness and to learn—and thus benefit—from the events of the day.

For therapists and counselors, a countertransferential review helps them get in touch with the feelings they have had in their treatment sessions. They seek to discover if their intense encounters with the persons they serve triggered distorted thoughts and beliefs. By looking at their own reactions, they not only learn things about themselves but also appreciate the people and situations they encounter in new ways.

For ministers, a theological reflection is a spiritual review of the day. In the process, they too stop at the end of the day to take stock of their lives. This, like the countertransferential review, helps them to catch the slide into unnecessary darkness and learn from difficult or intense events.

The process of theological reflection, which could be modified according to individual needs, includes the following steps:

~ Picking events during the day that stand out

~ Entering into the event and describing what happened (the objective) and how we felt (the subjective)

~ Avoiding the temptation to be discouraged, blame others (projection) or ourselves (self-condemnation); instead, see what we can learn

from the event about ourselves and our vulner-
abilities, needs, addictions, fears, anxieties,
worries, and desires

~ Reflecting on these learnings in light of what we
believe (our philosophy, ethics, and/or theology)

~ Deciding on how these learnings should change
us personally, interpersonally, professionally

~ Changing the way we behave

In the Buddhist tradition, Zen roshis teach that
feelings, past hurts, shame, questions, and needs will
come to the surface during meditation. These can
teach us if we are willing to pay attention to and
refrain from judging, blaming, indulging in, or reject-
ing our feelings. Instead, we must be open to learn
from these experiences as we would have others learn
from us. In his spiritually rich book *A Path With Heart,*
Jack Kornfield relates this point by way of a story
about his teacher:

Spiritual transformation is a profound process
that doesn't happen by accident. We need a
repeated discipline, a genuine training, in order
to let go of our old habits of mind and to find
and sustain a new way of seeing. To mature on
the spiritual path we need to commit ourselves
in a systematic way. My teacher, Achann Chah,
described this commitment as "taking the one
seat." He said, "Just go into the room and put
one chair in the center. Take the one seat in the
center of the room, open the doors and

windows, and see who comes to visit. You will witness all kinds of scenes and actors, all kinds of temptations and stories, everything imaginable. Your only job is to stay in your seat. You will see it all arise and pass, and out of this, wisdom and understanding will come."

We all can benefit from these processes—be it countertransferential review, theological reflection, or Buddhist meditation. People who wish to live truly aware lives need to take time out during the day or at day's end to quietly sit with their feelings in an objective, nonjudgmental way. The more we can do this on a regular basis, the more we can avoid unnecessary darkness and live through the unpleasant events of life in a way that provides direction and learning.

Debriefing ourselves also can be enhanced by sharing this process with someone we trust to accompany us on the psychological and spiritual journey. When we get feedback from those we trust, we will cut down on the distortion and discouragement that arises when we seek to be truly honest and loving with ourselves. The importance of having the patience and determination to go deeper in our lives sometimes can't be seen until someone else, much wiser than we are, helps nudge us along in the self-discovery process. A sensitive spiritual guide who was aware of the important role balance plays in exploring our inner life once told me this story which nicely illustrates my point:

As I reflected on Jesus' call to "Put out into the deep water and lower your nets for a catch (Lk 5:4)," a childhood memory came to mind. My aunt would advise me on how to draw a cup from a fresh pail of milk. The cream and froth would be gathering to the top, and if you put your mug in straight, it either filled with froth (no substance, shallow) or with all the cream (too rich for your system).

Instead she showed me how to bend over and blow gently on the top, about three gentle blows. The froth and cream would glide over to the sides and I could then put my mug in deep down and draw up milk and angle my cup in such a way to gather just a little cream as well.

Beautiful! But you had to be willing to patiently, gently, blow the froth and to reach into the depth and draw up a full, balanced catch.

A "full, balanced catch" involves discovering:

~ What we were *feeling* (affect) at different points in the day

~ What we were *thinking* that caused us to feel that way

~ What we were *believing* that made us think or come to the conclusions we arrived at.

Not to review and learn from our day is foolish. Moreover, if we don't constantly spend time asking ourselves about why we feel, think, and believe what we do, we will ruin the chance to live a freer, more satisfying life.

If we avoid looking at ourselves, we don't get a chance to uncover the hidden programming which may be driving us in directions we need not go. By taking the time to examine ourselves during the day and at day's end, we get a chance to cut the psychological strings being held by the "hidden puppeteer" (our unconscious or hidden erroneous beliefs) and live our lives in a clearer, more intentional way. Obviously, this is essential if we are to live a peaceful, full, and compassionate life.

Lesson 4

seek
hidden
possibilities

Dorothy Day, who cared for the poor for much of her adult life, was deeply concerned about the plight of others. She once said, probably with more than a tinge of frustration, "No one has the right to sit down and feel hopeless. There's too much to do."[4]

Given this, battling hopelessness in ourselves and avoiding unnecessary worrying is essential so we can both live fully and be there for others. We must take care of ourselves, prune away unhealthy motivations and intentions, and enjoy the renewing oases in our lives. But, beyond this we must be willing to sense life differently so we don't miss the possibilities that may seem hidden for the moment. The following remembrance of a spiritual counselor from Ireland, and a former student of mine, demonstrates this in a poignant way:

During what was a troubled time for me (I was about seven or eight) I visited with my aunt on her small farm. We walked together and came to a particular field. It was winter and frost covered the land. The ground beneath our feet was winter dark and hard.

She looked over at me, smiled, and asked me to kneel down, close my eyes, and place my hands on the earth. I did so and she said almost in a deep whisper, "Feel the life." I couldn't feel anything and told her so. She then told me to put my ear close to the earth and whispered hoarsely again, "Listen to the life." In response I put my head close to the earth and listened intently. But I heard nothing.

When I got up and told her that I could neither feel nor hear "the life," she took my face between her hands and said, "*alanna mo chroi* (child of my heart), it is often when the land seems most barren, cold, and dark that life is quietly growing!" When she said that, I knew she was also speaking to my inner pain and the need for hope during the winter I was experiencing at such a young age. Then, almost as an afterthought, she added as we turned to leave, "We will return again in the spring."

And when spring came, we did return. And as we came over the hill and I ran down the hill ahead of her, I could see that new tender life was shooting up. When she caught up to me, I turned to her and said, "You were right. You told me the truth!" In reply, she said nothing, just smiled, looked into my eyes, and drew out a smile from within my soul.

We also came again when the fruits of the soil were gathered. In this visit she spoke of the fact that this was the season of gathering the nourishment needed for the next "winter" and she said, "Remember *alanna*, to read the seasons. New possibilities, God, are in them all!"

The friendship this young Irish girl had with her aunt helped her to read the seasons in life and see their possibilities. It also demonstrated the role relationships play in helping us to keep a sense of perspective.

A number of years ago I was invited to guide a week-long retreat in Guatemala for persons dealing with very stressful situations. En route to Guatemala and at the request of Cardinal Joseph Bernardin, I stopped in Chicago to speak to his priests at their annual clergy gathering. I was glad to accept the Cardinal's invitation because the Catholic Archdiocese of Chicago has so many impossible needs and challenges that sometimes I get the feeling that it "eats its priests." So, anything I could do for them and Bernardin, whom I had long admired, was a privilege for me.

I also had two other positive and rather self-serving reasons for going. First, Chicago is one of my favorite cities. The people are great and I just can't get over a large, bustling city that actually has a beach bordering its downtown area. In addition, my new book was about to be published, and I hoped the Cardinal might be willing to write a brief pre-review for it if I asked him while I was there.

So, when I arrived and he greeted me with the statement that he was grateful I could take out the time to help him out, I saw my opportunity. I asked if he would be willing to write a brief pre-review for *Seeds of Sensitivity*. He said he would be glad to consider it and that I should send him a copy of the manuscript.

When I later gave my talk to the priests on the simple care of a hopeful heart, I could see by their faces that they were grateful. It was evident that the priests were genuinely appreciative of the fact that someone truly believed in them and was suggesting some simple ways they could keep their energy alive. The Cardinal himself was probably also in need of the psychological support since he had just been unjustly accused of sexual abuse and was undergoing great stress as well.

After the presentation, the Cardinal strode up to me and was obviously pleased. Smiling he said, "Bob, that was really good!"

I looked back at him, and teased him, "Well, you don't have to sound so surprised, Cardinal."

To which, he laughed, and added, "No. No kidding! It really was good."

He then quickly added, "You are going to send me that manuscript, aren't you?"

"Yes, if it is okay, I'd like to."

To which he responded, "Not only am I willing to do it, it would be an honor." Later that day in the Chicago airport, I called home and asked that a copy of the manuscript be sent to him. Then I went to Guatemala for a week's work.

Upon my return, much to my surprise, already sitting on my desk was the Cardinal's review and a cover letter. In it he said, "Enclosed is the review. I hope it is all right. But I want to tell you a little secret. Usually when people send me these manuscripts, I have my theologian read them first and draft a comment to which I can add my name. But in your case I want to assure you that I read every word."

Later in the year we had hoped to meet at my home for dinner and some good conversation. However, he got sick and died soon after, and so our social encounter never happened. But I have never forgotten his warm gesture.

I must admit that in my life it makes me happy to recall my successes. I get a kick out of them. I've worked really hard for everything, so I am proud of any achievements with which God has blessed me. However, it is in the midst of my failures that I feel things in the deepest way and have discovered the most lasting lessons. One of them is the value of small gestures of kindness and the need to resurrect them as a means of support when all seems lost.

The kind words and gestures of others are like buried treasure that we can find and explore whenever we need the gold of encouragement and an awareness of the presence of goodness in the world. The kind words of others help us regain perspective when all seems dark. They help us see that different possibilities are with us in every season of our lives.

William Sloane Coffin, the chaplain at Yale University, reflected upon this in his autobiography *Once to Every Man.* He related a story about problems in his marriage that were causing him to consider resigning from his position at Yale:

> To his surprise, Kingman Brewster (Yale's president) refused to accept his resignation. He and Brewster had not been seeing eye to eye on Coffin's controversial activities, and the resignation could have been a convenient way for Brewster to rid himself of his troublesome chaplain. Instead, he invited Coffin to move in with him and his wife.
>
> Still not satisfied that he should not resign, Coffin talked it over with his faculty colleague Richard Sewall. Sewall also advised against

resignation and gave him a compelling reason. "Bill," he said, "if you have suffered from anything, it is from an aura of too much success."[5]

Failures naturally aren't pleasing. No one wants them. However, the more we are involved in life, the more we can expect failure. So we'd better be able to put failure in perspective. Otherwise, we risk responding to failure with denial, avoidance, projection of blame onto others, burnout, or self-blame. These are not very good choices especially when failure and darkness can teach us so much if we are honest, patient, and remember the advice of Thomas Merton to a friend who was experiencing spiritual darkness: "Courage comes and goes . . . hold on for the next supply!"

Worrying Is a Waste, Concern a Compassionate Gift

We have such a small life. It really passes quickly. Yet, we often waste much of it by alternating between feelings of guilt for what we have or have not done, and being unnecessarily judgmental of others and their actions. When we are not experiencing these extremes, we fill most of the middle ground with periods of worry about what might happen in the future to us, our families, and others who are important in our life.

I know that people spend their time mired down in guilt, judgmental thinking, and worry because a great deal of my work involves helping people not to fret unnecessarily. The initial response I often get from people is that worrying is natural. Well, if this is so, then perhaps we need to practice being unnatural! Even if worry is the natural response, to continue along this vein of thinking is foolish. We can and need to do something about it.

Imaging powerful religious figures that model and teach the opposite is a good beginning. Buddha's serenity is an example. The Dalai Lama's constant smile is an inspiration. And how about Jesus' simple, challenging question: "What does it benefit you to worry? How will it change anything one iota?" Mark Twain also recognized the total foolishness of worrying when he wrote, "My life has been filled with terrible misfortunes . . . most of which never happened."

Once we have the image of serene spiritual figures in our hearts and keep words debunking the value of worrying at hand, we are ready for the next step. When we feel a sense of worry coming on, we need to catch ourselves and see how it hurts us and those around us as well. This conscience-jolter will encourage us to further appreciate that one of the greatest things we can share with others is a sense of our own peace. It will in turn further reinforce our desire not to give away our lives to worry.

When my daughter was ill in the hospital a number of years back, I would drive to visit her filled with "natural worry." On one of those visits, she looked up and saw my grim face, smiled slightly, and said, "Dad, you look worse off than I feel."

We both laughed. I lightened up after her comment. But it also woke me up to what I was doing. I was not only a burden to myself but to the very person I wanted to help.

Our culture encourages worry. It is as though worrying is the right thing to do. Somehow worrying is seen as something that will prevent or control terrible events. When my daughter was sick, the message I often got from the neighbors was: "If you are not always looking unhappy and burdened with crippling worry—and show it to us when we see you—it means you don't really care."

This is pure nonsense, of course. But I thought, why try to teach them differently? I have enough on my hands as it is. I remembered the old saying: "Don't attempt to teach a pig to sing. It wastes your time—and irritates the heck out of the pig." So, I would look grim as I left the house until I got out of the neighborhood. Then, I would turn on the radio, smile, look at the beautiful day before me as a gift from God. I listened to fun music as I drove so I would be refreshed and in a good state of mind when I arrived. I didn't want to appear tired or stressed but rather filled with a sense of peace so that I had something valuable to share.

I think we're all good at seeing the problems that surface in our lives. We also are pretty good at diagnosing what's causing them and planning what to do about them. Yet, few of us take the next step and simply do what we can with a sense of joy and freedom. Instead, we focus on how little or inefficient our actions are. Once we are done with recognizing, diagnosing, planning, and acting, very few of us remember to let go. After all, if we are spiritual people who've done what we can, shouldn't we then let God take care of the residue?

Worry is like a spiritual treadmill. It exercises the feeling of compassion. It is good in that it reminds us to care. However, as with a treadmill, worry doesn't really get us very far. Whereas, concern—which also wakes us up to the needs around us—is different in that it leads us to identify the appropriate actions we can take, then lets us relax and be at peace.

Worry is debilitating because it glues us to the problem. Concern, on the other hand, is freeing because it lets us sit alongside the issues, fears, sadness, losses, and uncontrollable and undesirable events that come our way. But letting go of worry is not so straightforward. Otherwise, so many people wouldn't worry so much.

A woman once questioned me at a presentation I gave. She was interested in the subject of "letting go." She tended to become preoccupied with, and inordinately worried about, a lot of things. "How do I let go?" she asked. "I've tried and nothing seems to work for me."

This is a natural problem. The Russian writer Maxim Gorky used to tell about a game he played with his brother. It simply involved the task of going into a corner and trying *not* to think about a white

bear. It revolved around the simple idea that the more
we try to let go of something, the more we become
tied to it. Just think of dieting. When we go on a diet,
we wind up thinking about the very thing we wish to
give up.

Diets, like worry, can wake us up to the need
for change. They can be the fuse to enkindle new
motivation to remove whatever addictions we have in
our lives. But in the long run, diets don't work. Food
dieters usually gain back all the weight they've lost, if
not more. Like dieters, worriers not only don't control
what troubles them but often wind up worse off.
Experiencing sleepless nights, and feeling overwhelmed, they often lose the joy in their own lives
and feel more futility than when they began their pre-
occupation with the problems in their lives.

Concern is a very different process. While it may
look like worrying, it is not paralyzing. It frees even
when the desired results are not achieved. Concern
doesn't deny there is a problem. It faces the issues
directly. However, it then musters the thought, "How
can I sit with this trouble in a good way?" Worry
encourages us to spend all our energy wringing our
hands over something. Concern looks at how we can
show mercy toward the issue or person involved and
thus respond with compassion.

This attitude of mercy, coupled with a spirit of
humility, is at the heart of true concern. It helps us to
determine, given our own limits, what we can
do about something. Maybe it is practiced with a

kind word. Possibly it is calling someone up and just listening to his or her problems without getting so distraught ourselves that we avoid contacting that person again.

And, if you think that "just listening" isn't a powerful gift, ask yourself about the last time you needed a kind ear. Did you have friends who heard you out? Did they do so without getting upset themselves? Or did they quickly respond with their answers to your problems?

Simple concern is quite powerful because it involves us in the problems of life without allowing us to get trapped by them. Let's use dieting as a metaphor again. People who constantly worry about food miss the rest of life. Whereas people concerned about living in a healthy, full way have an attitude that makes food enjoyable as but one gift of life among many. Rather than worrying about food, those concerned with healthy living eat a little less, eat a little more slowly, enjoy a sweet now and then, and walk a little more. These "littles" add up to a lot.

A little concern goes a long way. A lot of worry takes us nowhere.

So, the simple lesson here is that discerning between the two processes and making the transition from being a worrier to a concerned person is an enjoyable, intriguing, and worthwhile project to undertake. Reading the seasons and feeling the life will then result when we are better able to sense possibilities that may be hidden for the moment when life seems dark. At such times, hopeful attention and patience are truly good companions. Telling ourselves that even in the worst of times hidden growth is going on is one way to trigger an attitude that will allow these companions to help us see life in a new way when the timing is right.

Lesson 5

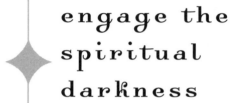

engage the spiritual darkness

most of the troubles we encounter are avoidable. Professional helpers and healers recognize this, practice ways to prevent their own slide into darkness, and try to teach us ways to avoid unnecessary suffering. However, sometimes the sense of helplessness, confusion, loneliness, and near despair we encounter at periods in our life is unavoidable. This spiritual darkness is not mere sadness, nor is it clinical depression, or the result of poor coping skills. It is an existential confrontation with ourselves, the human condition, and with what and how we believe about life, fate, and death. For some of us it is an existential confrontation with what we believe about God.

Spiritual darkness may have a very discernable precipitating event—loss of a spouse or dear friend, realizations of childhood sexual abuse, the dramatic decrease in the confidence others place in you, a parting of ways with a close friend, a serious illness, infidelity that undermines marital trust, a job loss, or repeated misunderstandings or hurtful comments by someone you love. These are only several of the more common triggers.

In some cases, the beginning of the darkness may be less obvious. In such instances, we find it hard to answer the question, "When did it begin?" Whatever the case, though, the more important factor is: recognizing spiritual darkness for what it is, namely, both a devastatingly lonely experience and an opportunity for new spiritual and psychological depth. Neither aspect should be underestimated. Spiritual darkness is an awful experience to encounter and go through. But, just as important, it is also an unasked for and unusual opportunity to be graced with radically new ways to relate to ourselves, others, even to life itself. There is a Persian proverb that sums it up well: "If life throws a knife at you, you can catch it by the blade or by the handle."

The question is will we recognize and take this opportunity, or will we only focus on the suffering and miss the opportunities for radical inner change that this spiritual experience offers? My sense is that most of us often don't let the possibilities blossom in the darkness. Instead, we hold on to our losses, run away, medicate ourselves (with work, alcohol, sex, religiosity), or live out of our bitterness in such a way that everything is tainted. We do none of this willfully or consciously. But the personal pain and the unlived joys and peace that could have developed with new learning (or maybe more accurately *un*learning) are nonetheless devastating.

One of the ways people are encouraged not to run away from life's necessary spiritual darkness is to help them see the benefits of staying the course. Some of those advantages are:

~ Increased motivation and determination to face the darkness in ourselves and others
~ Greater insight into one's personality style, defenses, values, gifts, spirituality, and areas of vulnerability
~ Less dependence on the recognition or approval of others
~ New skills and styles of behavior to complement our usual—possibly habitual—ways of interacting with others,
~ A sense of peace that is independent of external success, comfort, and security

In addition, since there are some negative situations and long-term impasses—such as racism and sexism—that can't be circumvented, why not let whatever possibilities emerge that can? By staying with our darkness with humility, openness, and what little courage we have, this is exactly what we are inviting—radical new possibility and necessary change for the next phase of our lives.

When spiritual writer and Oxford scholar Andrew Harvey was on a journey in India, he experienced a great deal of inner turmoil. Fortunately, he was also quite transparent and often surrounded by ordinary people of good faith. In his contemporary spiritual classic *A Journey in Ladakh,* one of them candidly appraised his situation and gave him this hopeful feedback:

> You smile a great deal and you listen well, but I see that somewhere you are sad. I see that nothing has satisfied you. . . . No, nothing has satisfied you, not your work, not your friendships, not all your learning and traveling. And that is good. You are ready to learn something new. Your sadness has made you empty; your sadness has made you open!

The same can be said of practically any negative emotion. Kathleen Norris in *Dakota*, for instance, notes that, "Fear is not a bad place to start a spiritual journey." Thomas Merton writes, "True love and prayer are learned when love becomes impossible and the heart has turned to stone." The question when confronted with any form of darkness is, will we stay the course or run, or seek a quick fix?

What Most People Do

Since spiritual darkness is most often viewed as a problem to be solved, most people's first—and false—start is to try harder. But the old maxim, "If at first you don't succeed, try, try again," doesn't work in this instance. It's like bargaining with God at the final stage of a terminal illness. It's like a person facing the darkness using logic, planning, and activities that have worked for them in the past. The only problem is, their efficient past approaches don't work this time.

Why? Because spiritual darkness is an unsolvable, permanent, and unwanted reality that must be faced directly, trusting that new possibilities are present but not yet seen.

If a family member dies or a friend breaches a trust, the clock can't be turned back. If your colleagues at work rightly or erroneously see you as failing, no amount of reasserting your position will convince them otherwise. As a matter of fact, behavior like this will probably be seen as defensive and make the situation worse. And, this is exactly what our normal problem-solving approach does in situations involving true spiritual darkness. Our well-meant, usually effective steps make us feel even more helpless. What a mess.

We finally recognize trying harder, bargaining with God, or doing anything to return life to normal (pre-darkness) as false starts. We realize they won't succeed. Often we react with deep sadness, helplessness, and feelings of failure, shame, and anger. But possibly the worst part of all is that in this spiritual place, we feel alone and terribly lost.

This sense of being lost is not a pinpoint experience but usually lasts over a long period of time. During this time we are fearful, distraught, and filled with self-questioning. At several points throughout this period of darkness we find ourselves faced with the choice to:

~ Continue trying approaches that have worked in the past even though they are not succeeding now;

~ Run away from the darkness through denial, rationalization, or minimization;

~ Medicate ourselves through work, drugs, sex, excessive religiosity, or some other compulsive behavior; or

~ Face the darkness directly with a sense of trust that life will provide a new way for us—even if at some level we doubt this!

This last option is obviously not an easy one. We want what we want. We want a return to life as it was before a crisis triggered the darkness. Or we want our usual way of coping and regaining equilibrium or mastery to work. But, whether we like it or not, this is not to be.

If and when we finally recognize this fully, along with recognizing our fragility, helplessness, alienation, deep sadness, and being lost, surprisingly we will experience a sense of peace. When we can no longer support our frantic flailing efforts at control and self-justification, we must either surrender in trust or remain lost forever.

In 2002 I was working on self-care with the priests of Boston at the height of the pedophilia scandal. I framed my presentations under the heading of spiritual darkness. The third and final day of these presentations was for retired priests, and it occurred on the heels of a revelation that one of the highest prelates of the diocese had been removed from ministry because of seemingly credible accusations. Those attending my presentation appeared deeply demoralized by this latest bombshell.

Just as I was about to wrap up the question and answer period, a man on the right side of the room shot up his hand to squeeze in one last question. "I want to divinize you for a moment." I replied, "This sounds dangerous!" and smiled.

He laughed, and then when the smile faded from his face he asked, "If you could predict the future, would you venture a guess as to when all of this will end?"

I looked at him and replied, "Even if I were divine and could answer your question, I wouldn't."

"Why?" he asked quite surprised.

"Because although the concern is a natural one, when you are in spiritual darkness, it is the wrong question. A more helpful one is: 'Given all of this darkness in me and in the diocese, what can I learn?'"

Surrendering in trust to God or believing in the personal value of asking questions and going to psychological places that we'd like to avoid is the point at which the futile cognitive, logical, left-brained efforts finally subside. Then the imaginative, new paradigm, right-brained way of perceiving allows new possibilities to rise.

It is, of course, quiet times that facilitate this movement. Sitting zazen—that is sitting alone or with a group in silent meditation—gives us the space to be in the darkness without preconceived notions of what would be the good, what would be the healing, or what would be the next move to take. In her classic article, "Impasse and the Dark Night of the Soul," the American Catholic nun Constance FitzGerald put it in these terms:

> It is precisely as broken, poor, and powerless that one opens oneself to the dark mystery of God in loving, peaceful waiting. When the pain of human finitude is appropriated with consciousness and consent and handed over in one's own person to the influence of Jesus' spirit in the contemplative process, the new and deeper experience gradually takes over, the new vision slowly breaks through, and the new understanding and mutuality are progressively experienced.

> At the deepest levels of night, in a way one could not have imagined it could happen,

one sees the withdrawal of all one has been certain of and depended upon for reassurance and affirmation.[6]

The American Buddhist nun Pema Chödrön, in her book *When Things Fall Apart*, addressed this need to directly face all of our life, including those places we naturally want to avoid. She says, "The trick is to keep exploring and not bail out, even when we find out something is not what we thought . . . [a] sign of health is that we don't become undone by fear and trembling, but we take it as a message that it's time to stop struggling and look directly at what's threatening us."

In my own case, one of the immediate benefits I found in surrendering and trusting in God and facing my own darkness was the ability to be able to enjoy "the now" more. For years I had spent much time in nostalgia or past regrets or resentments on the one hand, and planning for the future on the other. Little time was spent where I was, in the now.

In my deepest spiritual darkness, the now was the only place to go or be. Just when I started projecting myself into the future, I was hit by another wave of realization as to how I had failed others again and again in big and little ways. I had nowhere to go or hide. The only place to be was in the now and to experience life as best as I could.

Another benefit of this particular dark experience for me—which I think is characteristic of all darkness—was the realization that life is chronic. I knew at that moment that my darkness would never totally leave me. As a professional helper, I had been conditioned to see life and its problems as "acute." By that I mean, when challenges arose, I was trained to assess them, develop a program of treatment, and then apply them to conquer the problem and move on.

In many instances, this very cognitive, left-brained approach made sense. It still does. But there are times when this approach isn't appropriate. As a matter of fact, to use it during spiritual darkness or when facing the existential realities of life, death, and imperma-nence (all things change no matter what we do) is delusional.

Yet, most of us live by this delusion, and when it collapses in the darkness, we deny, ignore, or run away from the new wisdom sitting there. We don't see life as being filled with joys and chronically unsolv-able problems. However, if and when we do allow this delusion to melt away in the darkness, we can enjoy life's gifts and face its pains in ways that don't hold on to unnecessary suffering for any longer than is necessary.

One of the lessons learned in the darkness is that we must face *all* of our life with trust and courage. We must do this until it no longer takes courage because we realize that we can hold on. Life can only be appreciated for what it is, as it is now. And although society, with all its games and schemes, would have us think this is defeatist, it is far from the truth. While others read from menus of what they feel they deserve or need, by living in the now we can enjoy the actual food we have in front of us. If we can improve the meal, great. If we can make it different, great. But, by being grateful, trusting, and open in the now, we never ruin the meal we are being served now. The greatest gift of all is to never miss the joys and grandeur of the life that is before us each day.

Moreover, spiritual darkness—when it is fully embraced and allowed to teach us lessons we wouldn't learn if we were willfully in control—helps us to embrace the following essential lessons:

~ Learning takes place when we join clarity and kindness.

~ Great love is usually found in small deeds—not dramatic gestures or achievements.

~ We must toughen our souls so we can deal with things that upset us even though they really shouldn't.

~ We need to travel light by erecting a "barrier of simplicity" between ourselves and the world.

~ We need to come home to ourselves more often in a spirit of meditation and know why we sometimes avoid this beautiful prayer experience in our lives. (And, no, it's not because we are too busy!)

It is to these powerful lessons that we now turn.

Lesson 6

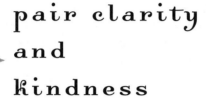

pair clarity and kindness

Anne Lamott, writing in *Traveling Mercies,* offered the following moving reflection on her minister:

There would be different pastors along the way, none of them exactly right for us until a few years ago when a tall African-American woman named Veronica came to lead us. She has huge gentle doctor hands, with dimples where the knuckles should be, like a baby's fists. She stepped into us, the wonderful old worn pair of pants that is St. Andrew, and they fit. She sings to us sometimes from the pulpit and tells us stories of when she was a child. She told us this story just the other day: When she was about seven, her best friend got lost one day. The little girl ran up and down the streets of the big town where they lived, but she couldn't find a single landmark. She was very frightened. Finally a policeman stopped to help her. He put her in the passenger seat of his car, and they drove around until she finally saw her church. She pointed it out to the policeman, and then she told him firmly, "You could let me out now. This is my church, and I can always find my way home from here."

And that is why I have stayed so close to mine—because no matter how bad I am feeling, how lost or lonely or frightened, when I see the faces of the people at my church, and hear their tawny voices, I can always find my way home.

Such "tawny voices" of which Lamott speaks hold both kindness and clarity. If we just have kind people around us, we can become complacent, narcissistic, and uncritical of ourselves. If we only have people who clarify the growing edges in our behavior without accompanying kindness, we may feel overwhelmed and disheartened. It's only natural for negative realities to pull us down before we discover their benefits.

Kindness

Kindness is essential for clarity to effect change. This is especially the case in regard to the love and gentleness with which we treat ourselves. Self-awareness and self-love go hand in hand. Kenneth Leech states in his book *True Prayer*, "You do not want to know someone whom you despise, even if, especially if, that someone is you."

Self-love is manifested in many ways. Chief among them is the act of kindness toward ourselves. The problem is that all of us—maybe especially professional healers, helpers, and compassionate individuals—find it easier to be kind to others than to ourselves. The last thing many of us think about is a way to be as gentle with ourselves as we are with others.

Once I was mentoring a very dedicated and accomplished clinical social worker who was having a great deal of turmoil in his personal life. After we had walked for about an hour and wound our way back to the car and bade our goodbyes, he thanked me for my listening ear. I acknowledged his gratitude. Then just as he was getting into the car, a thought hit me and I said by way of closure, "You know, Jack, given all you are going through, even though you are a therapist and are responsible for others, it's okay to feel sorry for yourself once in a while."

He seemed surprised at first. Then his eyes filled up. He paused, smiled, and after a long moment of silence said, "Your comment means more to me than I can even describe."

Even when we hit bottom, the bounce up from the cellar can bring with it new healthy insights and behaviors not previously in our repertoire. It can also bring newfound energy. I think Anne Morrow Lindberg was right when she said: "The most exhausting thing in life, I have discovered, is being insincere." However, we must remember to be *both* kind and clear with ourselves. When the element of being gentle with ourselves is absent, the results can be terrible. I have seen this in many instances with those in the helping and healing professions with whom I have worked.

During one of my own tough times, I would quietly look out the window, feeling tired, lost, and alone. For a while, I choked with sadness; then after a period, just a quiet numbness remained. It was as if I had woken up after a long sleep or illness, still not fully alert, just there. Then slowly I seemed to feel the energy return to my spirit, but it was still somehow muted.

I had always been an intense person, a pleaser who aimed high and liked success, and one who has a sense of self-importance and is fairly self-centered as well. As I moved up after hitting bottom, I was sure I was still all those things, but somehow the sense of failure had softened my soul.

Success now seemed like a fun thing, not really necessary for my deep peace or sense of joy. Pleasing others also changed in a small significant way. I still wanted to be kind to others. I think I might have felt even more able to be compassionate. But I was now able to combine clarity with kindness more deftly because of my own experience of feeling like a failure. Rather than using confrontation as a tool, I would more gently describe the state of affairs and let a clear description of the situation nudge others to see the situation and decide what, if anything, they wanted to do.

However, even more significant, my sense of failure took the edge off my own fears of letting people down. Maybe for the first time in my life, I felt my own real limits. I knew that I was trying about as hard as I could to be the best person possible. I was writing as honestly as I could. I was putting my family and close friends first. I was trying to support my colleagues at work as best I could. My own work seemed to reflect my desire to share my heart as well as I was able.

Interestingly enough, people sometimes didn't seem to take notice. While I felt a period of purity of heart in my intentions and efforts to be compassionate and open up a space for people to feel welcome, some continued to question my efforts. Others would remind me in subtle ways how, in comparison with others, my efforts did not measure up. The Yiddish proverb kept coming to mind: "Sleep faster . . . we need the pillows!"

The strange thing for a pleaser like me, though, was that their hurtful reactions didn't completely crush me. I knew I had and still failed miserably at times. Even though I liked myself and was doing some good things, I knew I was still quite limited in so many ways. Paradoxically, I felt more limited now than ever, yet I knew I was doing better than ever!

This unusual awareness and feeling gave me a quiet confidence that sat alongside the ever-present residue of sadness I felt from the memories of my failures in life. I knew, for my own sake, as well as that of my family, friends, colleagues, and others who relied on me, that I couldn't let the views and expectations of others completely crush me. After all, what would that accomplish?

Maybe for the first time in my life I saw myself as the little boy who wanted to run down the baseline and score, only to trip short of home plate. I picked him up this time, dusted him off, smiled at him, and said, "great hit." In that moment of imagery I knew I was going to be okay. I knew this not because I succeeded, not because everyone would be happy with my efforts, but because I knew I wanted to be a better person than ever before. And with the love of God, family, and friends, I was going to do it. Beyond that, for the first time I really understood what Arthur Schopenhauer intended in his warning, "We forfeit three-fourths of ourselves in order to be like other people." I recognized myself what I had been teaching others for years. Too often in an effort to be a better person, we only wind up trying to be another person—a sure recipe for continued failure and a sense of "lostness."

Clarity

With kindness, then, we can move further along in looking at both the pleasant and unpleasant in our lives. However, as essential as kindness is, it must be joined by courageous clarity. As the person in the following lyrical story recognized, we can and need to move more deeply in our life even when we want to pull back. Even when it hurts, we need to seek as much clarity about our lives as possible.

> My mother asked me to prepare her two front barrels for summer plants. I knew this meant weeding out the old dry spring plants and adding new fertilizer to the soil.
>
> I did what I thought was a good job, and proudly announced in a loud voice, "I'm finished!"
>
> She came up beside me and poked her garden stick into the barrels. She smiled, nudged me, and in a lilting voice teased, "Well, my heavens, you're like a hen; you've only just scratched around on the surface."
>
> When I looked at her with a question on my face, she put her arm around me, pointed to the soil, and advised, "Dig down deep and shake up the soil. In this way, you will allow the air to get

through and you will be getting the fertilizer to mix down deep in the soil where it's needed."

She also took out her new plants and prepared them for me by shaking the life out of the tightly bound roots. Reading my look of concern over this "rough treatment," she smiled in a gentle wise way and said, "Shaking up can be very good for growth." Then as I set off to industriously and meticulously follow her advice, she added as she walked away, "Think especially about this last bit as you do the job."

I knew what she meant. I had been having a tough time of it as of late. In response I had avoided the pain and traumatic changes that had occurred over the past year. So, as I worked my hands down deep into the soil, making room, creating space, and shaking the roots of the plants before placing them where they needed to be to grow, my tears softened the soil. I felt strongly that both the plants and I would do well and that pain can be a transition to new life if it isn't avoided or feared.

Clarity helps us see what we are avoiding, holding on to, or fearing. Such attachments, worries, and daily idols are evident when we feel the emotions of anger, depression, or stress. They point to difficult situations, losses to be grieved, and areas in our life where we have stubbornly proclaimed: "If I don't have _____" or "If this person doesn't feel _____ about me, I can't be happy."

Of course, having preferences is not a bad thing. Being seen in a good light by others or having many talents and few growing edges or blind spots is naturally enjoyable. But our image and possessions are not everything. As a matter of fact, we need to risk them all if we are to be honest and free. Like little children, we must call it like it is rather than covering up.

When my daughter was only four years old, the electricity went out in our apartment building. It was a nice day, and rather than staying inside, my wife decided to take Michaele to the park. This meant walking down from the eighth floor since the elevator was not working.

As they entered the stairwell, my daughter hesitated because it was dark. When she halted, my wife asked her why. She responded, "There may be monsters down there!" To which my wife replied, "There aren't any monsters in this building." Then after a brief pause my daughter retorted, "How do *you* know; you can't see either!"

Clarity involves simplicity and directness. It doesn't hide behind complex defensiveness or excuses. To counteract our tendency to avoid the truth, we need to be aware of the temptation to project the blame (that's arrogance), beat ourselves up (that's ignorance), or expect results in self-awareness and growth too quickly (that's discouragement).

Instead of being arrogant, ignorant, or discouraged, we need to be faithful to seeking clarity. But we need to pace ourselves as well. As the fourth-century desert monk Abba Macarius advised: "Don't try to understand everything—take on board as much as you can and try to make it work for you. Then the things that are hidden will be made clear to you."[7]

Clarity requires we slow down our lives for meditation and reflection. Most often we swallow the day's activities whole without tasting the experiences or appreciating the interactions.

By changing the pace of our lives and ensuring we have a bit of time for reflection and meditation, we will be able to see through the negative training and habits that have disabled us. Writing in *The Tibetan Book of Living and Dying,* Sogyal Rinpoche rightly recognizes:

> We are already perfectly trained . . . trained to get jealous, trained to grasp, trained to be anxious and sad and desperate and greedy, trained to react angrily to whatever provokes us. We are trained . . . to such an extent that these negative emotions rise spontaneously, without our even trying to generate them. . . .

> However if we devote the mind in meditation to the task of freeing itself from illusions, we will find that with time, patience, discipline, and the right training, our mind will begin to unknot itself and know the essential bliss and clarity.

Honesty with ourselves is very difficult even when we proclaim loudly that we are open. However, the danger that self-delusion brings—even in little things—will cause us great difficulties. The African proverb is correct: "Not to know is bad; not to wish to know is worse."

The goal of clarity is to see ourselves honestly—but also kindly. In doing this, we will not spiritually sink under guilt for past sins or be pulled psychologically into the past. But instead, with a sense of courageous clarity, we will have true remorse for past errors so that we may learn from them in order to live differently and to live with greater dignity and compassion. Kindness and clarity paired is a true recipe for wisdom.

The challenging lesson for us is: Are we balancing the two of them? If we are not, then what do we do to increase either clarity or kindness so the mixture is better? Such a simple, but often overlooked, step allows us to quickly adjust our attitude toward ourselves and others in a way that can have immediate positive results.

Lesson 7

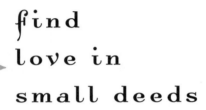

find love in small deeds

In addition to being kind to ourselves, we also need to open up to the gentle presence of others in our lives. There are so many people who, during the day, care for us through little words of affirmation or other small ways. But we take them all for granted and miss the power of their wonderful support.

It may take the form of family and friends saying a kind word. They may call just to let us know they are thinking of us. Or, they may do a small chore for us so we don't have to do it ourselves. Often these are unrecognized graces. We fail to recognize them because we are used to them, maybe too used to them. Then we miss them when they are gone.

Being grateful for the wonderful people in our lives now would certainly change our behavior toward them. As in the case of all graces, it would benefit us as well as them. With an appreciation of the kindness that is around us, we can be clearer about what we need to improve about ourselves without being pulled down by those realizations. We can also feel as loved as we truly are by the people already present in our lives. They provide touchstone experiences to remind us that we are not alone.

A teacher once told me the following story about her high school days that I think illustrates my point.

I was a sophomore in high school and played on the girl's basketball team. Being insignificant sophomores, our practice time was scheduled from 8:00 to 10:00 at night. I lived relatively close to school, so after practice every night I had to walk home in the dark, and I hated it. I hated it because I had to walk up this long, steep, dimly lit hill that had a thick wooded area to the left of it. Even though the neighborhood was very safe, as I walked past the woods I always imagined that someone was in there watching me and waiting to attack me. I could work myself up pretty well with these thoughts. So often I would go home and plead with my mother, "Can't someone come and pick me up?"

Her answer always was, "No." My father was taking night classes at the time and my mother worked a night shift so the car just wasn't there. I was so bothered by the situation that I considered quitting the team and I told her. My mother would always respond, "Don't quit just because you're afraid." So I continued to go to practice and I continued to complain until one night when I was at practice we had a torrential rainstorm.

This particular evening as we were finishing up our final drills my dad came walking through the gym doors. When I met up with him I said, "Dad, what are you doing here?" And he said, "My class finished early because of the heavy rain. So, I thought I'd come and pick you up." I was delighted, so I grabbed my stuff and we headed out the door, got in the car—and eventually drove up the infamous dark hill.

As we drove about halfway up the hill we both noticed someone standing at the top of the hill. As we got closer we noticed that it wasn't a stranger, it was my mother! So I jumped over the seat into the back as my dad rolled down his window a little bit. Then, when we got closer to my mom my father stuck out his head and asked, "What are you doing out in the rain?" My mom quietly replied, "I'm waiting for Cindy." From the back seat I yelled, "Mom, I'm right here, get in the car."

When she got into the car I quietly asked, "Why were you waiting for me?" And I'll never forget what her answer was. She said: "I know that you don't like to walk past the woods at night, so I thought if you saw me standing here as you climbed the hill in the dark, you wouldn't be afraid." I sat in the back seat stunned. In this torrential rainstorm, my mother came out to be with me so I wouldn't be afraid. All that kept going through my mind was, "I really am loved! Not just by my parents, but I am truly loved by God." It was a depth of knowing that came from that experience that I had never felt before, and I felt so alive.

This experience remains as clear and powerful in my mind today as the day it happened eighteen years ago. It is a touchstone for me. Something I can reach back into and be reminded of God's loving presence in my life, especially during those times when the sun seems to set and the darkness prevents me from moving on, and I am tempted to fall asleep . . . and to forget.

It's as easy to forget that we are loved as it is to miss the precious daily opportunities to love others, particularly when we are preoccupied with our own problems. To illustrate, Mother Teresa once told the following story:

One night a man came to our house and told me, "There is a family with eight children. They have not eaten for days."

I took some food with me and went. When I came to that family I saw the faces of those little children disfigured by hunger. There was no sorrow or sadness in their faces, just the deep pain of hunger. I gave the rice to the mother. She divided the rice in two, and went out, carrying half the rice. When she came back, I asked her, "Where did you go?" She gave me this simple answer, "To my neighbors; they are hungry also!" I was not surprised that she gave—poor people are really very generous. I was surprised that she knew they were hungry. As a rule, when we are suffering, we are so focused on ourselves, we have no time for others."[8]

As a matter of fact, even when we are confronted by the difficulties of others, we often get so quickly lost in our own schedules, needs, and little problems, that we can't respond in a generous, genuine, and helpful way. This is very sad because we are capable of so much good. And when we are self-less and other-focused, we feed the good-heartedness in ourselves in a subtle but rich way. People who are truly sensitive to others find their hearts filled with peace and joy. But it's so easy to miss these chances. We run on automatic, acting and speaking out of self-interest without even recognizing it.

Surprisingly, this is more a sin of the wealthy than the poor; more apt to be a fault of the religious elite than those of simple faith. A number of years ago my wife needed immediate surgery for a serious illness. Because of it, I needed to cancel a speaking engagement to a religious gathering to be with her. To let the conference organizer know, I called the main conference office. The telephone operator told me I would have to call Baltimore where the conference was being held. I did, and there was no response. So I called the woman back and decided to tell her the problem that necessitated the contact. In response, the telephone operator gave me a group of phone numbers so I was sure to get someone. But before I got a chance to thank her and hang up so I could try to get through to the conference organizer, the operator said in a quiet voice accented by a southern Washington, D.C. lilt: "I'm sorry for your troubles." I was deeply moved by her concern—especially since I really needed support even though I'm a professional helper.

After hanging up, I dialed the first number on the list and got through immediately. Relieved, I introduced myself, told to the woman who answered I would have to cancel my talk because I needed to be with my wife who was having surgery. She said: "Oh, you'd better speak to one of the persons in charge."

When that person got on the line, I told my story. She was clearly distressed and responded, "Oh my, oh my. . . ." She paused and I thought she was going to add a word or two of consolation. Instead she said, "You know, we've advertised your appearance really widely." I was stunned—too shocked in fact to respond by saying something nasty or sarcastic. I could understand her thinking something like that, but to actually say it to someone whose wife is going into surgery stunned me. So instead I quickly mumbled, "Well, it can't be helped," and hung up.

Later in reflection and prayer, I felt my anger rising. I also sensed God gently chiding me, leading me to an awareness that I had done worse when people needed my support. Instead of anger, I needed to have compassion for the woman who had missed the chance for "a caring moment." As a matter of fact, only two months later when a colleague couldn't review something I had written because her mother had been rushed to the emergency room, I responded just as dismally. Rather than feeling compassion for her, I felt disappointment for myself. For a few fleeting seconds I even thought, "Well maybe she can look through the manuscript in the hospital waiting room." Amazing!

How sad when we miss opportunities to encourage and support each other because we are lost in our own world of tasks and agendas. To dismiss such chances is to fail to be awake to the real challenge of true good-heartedness. Feeling and sharing both joys and sorrows in our lives is a good and simple challenge—but unfortunately because of our compulsive conditioning, it is not a very easy one to meet. This is sad because the combination of good support from friends and a deep, dynamic relationship with God can help us to move through even the darkest moments in ways we never expected.

In the following written reflection by a pastoral counseling student who lost her child after a long illness, we can see how her view of God became more rich and dynamic. We can also see how her appreciation of her fellow students set the stage for her to deepen her own compassionate nature—not in spite of her own pain but because of it.

> One Lenten season when I was struggling with my daughter's illness, I tried to focus on Christ's sacrifice. As I drove along I prayed, "Thank you God for sending your son to die for me." In less than a moment I was answered with, "Thank you for taking care of Becky." It was a very real moment and I know it was the Holy Spirit who spoke within me. I will never forget the split-second feeling I had of God's vulnerability. It came and went so quickly it was almost as if it hadn't happened. He was trusting me to take care of one of his own lambs. When I meditate on that time now I find myself asking, "What was it like for God when my daughter died?" I had never considered that before. I am still not ready to explore that question in any depth. When I can, I know it will increase my understanding of God's vulnerability and humility.

She then went on to write:

Although I am looking forward to my graduation, the feeling of accomplishment I associate with that day is coupled with a sadness that I will be leaving behind the weekly opportunities to be with others who are in the Loyola College Pastoral Counseling "community." In *Compassion*, the authors (Nouwen, McNeill, and Morrison) point out that "faith in God's compassionate presence can never be separated from experiencing God's presence in the community to which we belong." I realize that I will need to make a conscious effort to retain and add to the ties to others in the community of caring that I have benefited from at Loyola. The presence of community, along with continually seeking to know myself better and knowing the presence of the Holy Spirit's wisdom and guidance, are what enable me to be present to others.

Her insights into new understandings of herself, God, and others would all be needed in her work with others in the days to come. However, in reaching this point, she didn't realize how soon and personal her challenge would be to do this in her own family. She continued:

On Good Friday, 2001, my cousin called me, distraught and confused, to tell me that her six-week-old granddaughter had died that morning. This tiny new person had been sleeping between her parents and was apparently accidentally smothered. I listened and then asked what I could do. I was asked to help with funeral and cemetery arrangements as we had done this for our own child. On Saturday morning as I drove to meet my cousin and her son and his wife at the cemetery, I tried to think of what to bring to them. What would comfort them? What I had was myself and that, I decided, was the best gift I could give them. I found myself praying, "Lord, be present in my presence as I am with these grieving parents and this baby's grandmother. Holy Spirit, help me to know how to be truly present to them." I learned on that day that I was stronger than I thought I was, I have more to offer than I thought I did; and that writing this paper has enabled me to pull together a lot of loose ends in my spiritual beliefs, enabling me to see where the source of my strength and renewal originates. I can't do the work of pastoral counseling alone but, thank God, I don't have to do it on my own.

She recognized in this moment that when she absorbed the love of God and her family and friends in new ways each day, even in the most difficult situations, she was and is enough. When we realize and live this way, we are all enough. Our own experiences and memories of kindness and love to us will bear out the lesson. Great love is more often found in small deeds done than large actions about which we only dream. By remembering this when we are called to give or are privileged to receive some gestures of love, we will not step back but make the most of them.

Lesson 8

seek perspective daily

Years ago I met a fascinating negative character. She wasn't a depressive, but—as they say
today—she certainly was a carrier! She was a
true silver lining looking for a cloud. However, if you
were careful not to be pulled into meeting her
demands or wanting to force her to enjoy life, you
could see she had many wonderful traits.

By not personalizing her intermittent negative
comments, and through the use of humor, I was able
to actually enjoy her inner beauty. I didn't try to show
her how much she was missing by not being more
grateful and energetic. Her family repeatedly attempt-
ed this and only ended up being frustrated and quietly

resentful of her. Instead, I simply stood back a little and let her be herself. Then, I would let her know I realized the trouble she was having. She responded to this by being grateful to me for appreciating her plight.

Because I didn't try to "fix" her, we enjoyed one another as much as we could. By having a little distance from her constant negative comments and by decreasing the expectations I might normally have for someone truly interested in change, I did not often get pulled into her negative cloud. When I did—because she was a master at making people feel guilty—I just woke myself up to the fact that I wasn't on my guard, laughed at myself, and tried again. Actually, by making it into a game like that, it even turned out to be fun.

Later I helped her family to enjoy her more as well. I had to use a rather strange technique so they could see it as a game themselves. I told them that when they went to visit her or chatted on the phone with her (she was the mom), they had to see this encounter as if they were speaking to someone whom they didn't know. They needed to distance themselves. Also, they needed to act as if they were speaking to someone who had been committed for long-term treatment and who was not in touch with reality at all. In this way they would have no expectations that their mother was going to be able to comfort or respond positively to them as much as they would have loved such a response. With constant practice, the negative bonds were broken and most of the time they were able to be present to their mother in a way that didn't hurt them yet allowed their mother to get the attention she needed. By pruning their expectations, their availability was richer, less destructive, and more rewarding to all involved.

Persons in the helping professions also at times lose distance and are temporarily swept away by the expectations, needs, painful experiences, and negativity of others. More than most people, they are confronted with negativity and sadness. Yet, they are educated to pick up these signs as early as possible so they are not unnecessarily dragged down. We can learn much from how they avoid losing perspective or regain it when they temporarily lose their way. The distance they value can help us deal with the pain of others.

There is much benefit to remembering the Russian proverb: "When you live next to the cemetery, you can't cry for everyone who dies." Most of us, whether we are professional helpers or not, tend to personalize too much. We absorb the sadness, anxiety, and negativity of those around us. Sometimes we even feel this is expected of us. We sense that if we don't cry when our children fail, if we don't get stressed out by our spouse's temporary unhappiness, if we don't feel paralyzed by the injustices in society, then we think others—or perhaps ourselves—will believe we just don't care.

All caring people must come to grips with the danger of being negatively infected by those they support. Otherwise, their supportive presence will not only become too stressful to continue, but they will also face burnout and negativity in their interactions with the very persons for whom they are caring. Knowing the information professional helpers utilize is especially helpful. To set the stage, there are three basic principles to remember:

1. *Everyone gets overwhelmed once in a while.* That's natural. However, when we have a pattern of being pulled down, we need to change our perspective on how we relate to others, or it will become habitual.

2. *Caring means being willing to keep enough distance* from those we love or are concerned with so we are able to avoid drowning with them in their problems. This takes a willingness to forgo the "luxury of being upset" while a person is sharing his or her problem.

3. *Knowing the signals of over-involvement helps avoid burnout.* Recognizing our "red flags of emotion" before things get out of control is essential. Otherwise, we step over an emotional cliff, arguing or crying with someone when a clear head is really what is needed. This would be a wonderful gift to offer those we are trying to support.

Everyone Gets Overwhelmed Once in a While

Knowing we make mistakes at times relieves us of the temptation to erect new protective boundaries and in the process possibly make the situation worse. When people know they should keep a distance (so they are not pulled into another's pain) but still get drawn in, they sometimes complicate matters by how they react. They either pick on themselves for getting caught into a web of anger and stress, or they blame the other person for upsetting them. For example, a parent allows herself to be pulled into an argument with a teenage daughter, then later blames both herself and her child for losing her temper. As she ruminates about it for the rest of the day, she swings between guilt and self-recrimination on the one hand, and resentment of her daughter on the other.

The reality is that no matter how much experience we have even as professional helpers, we all get drawn in once in awhile. The important thing is to try to learn from it each time it happens and to:

1. Recognize the emotional signals—anger, sadness, fear, anxiety, feeling overwhelmed, pity—and to take a step back. For example, be quiet or excuse yourself for a moment, even leave the room to get some distance.

2. Don't condemn yourself or the other person who is probably also experiencing similar negative emotions about the encounter. Instead be curious about your reactions so you can learn from them and gain power over how you react in the future.

3. Try to figure out what the early signals are of being drawn in so you can see how you may improve your interactions in the future.

Forgo the "Luxury of Being Upset" While a Stressful Interaction Is Underway

Being upset is easy. Practically all of us can get teary-eyed at a sad movie. However, having the discipline to keep enough distance from the emotions of the moment is a real gift to those who turn to us for help and support. Once a coworker stepped into my office while I was sitting down chatting with a visitor. She told us a story about a terrible tragedy in her life. While my visitor got very upset, I tried to step back, listen to her, figure out how I could stand with her, and give her some clear feedback.

After she left, my visitor asked how I could hear the story and not get upset. I told him that she really saw his caring in the fact that he felt for her. But I saw my role as trying to help, much as a surgeon would in an operation. Each of us—in a different way—supported her.

"But weren't you upset?" he persisted.

"Yes, I was. But when I started to get upset, I told myself to put my feelings on hold until this evening when I could sit and think with them." By doing this I felt I could not only be helpful to her but I could reflect later on the feelings I had. Then, at a better time and in a safer place, I could let them move away from me so I didn't push them down or get caught in them in the future.

Pick Up the "Red Flags" of Our Emotions

The sooner we experience and note our emotional reactions, the greater the possibility we won't be drawn in or pulled down by them. Too often we don't do this because we think the external event is what is causing the reaction. This leads to foolish thinking that often causes us problems and doesn't lead to new information that might help us. If someone cuts us off on the highway, he or she is demonstrating inappropriate and dangerous behavior. But how much more foolish are we when we respond with anger and raised blood pressure? Yet, people do this all the time and feel it is a natural reaction. Well, it may be common—but it's also crazy.

The more we use our reactions to learn how we are giving away power, the more vital we will become. The ultimate goal in picking up our red flags of emotion is to change our spontaneous negative reactions into spontaneous neutral ones. When we do this, we will save energy, be in a more receptive place to learn about ourselves, and live a life where both positive and negative events can be greeted as teachable moments.

No one likes moments of stress and anxiety. Nor do we enjoy emotions such as anger, resentment, or sadness. The general tendency is to react to them by withdrawing, blaming, being overly cautious, or becoming discouraged. When this occurs again, allow the emotions to be signals of potential teachable moments. This can be done by:

~ Seeing the signals of distress we are experiencing.
~ Distancing ourselves by observing ourselves and the event as if it were happening to someone else.
~ Avoiding blame of self or others.
~ Asking how one can learn about oneself from these experiences.

Incorporating a learning paradigm for distressful moments is a proven method therapists use with themselves and also teach their clients. It is an approach spiritual guides employ to help their followers or directees recognize their attachments (for example, their image, being liked, or having wealth). In this way, we can see the cost of this silent slavery and can continue on the road to true freedom and a life of less stress and suffering.

Lesson 9

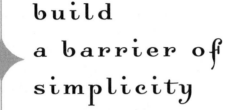

build
a barrier of
simplicity

f there is one word worth recalling with respect to the inner life it is "simplicity". Too often we are overwhelmed and confused by the very spiritual and psychological lessons that are designed to help us. Every time this happens to me, I remember the simple sane attitude of a small businessman who came to the United States from Italy many years ago.

He had three grown children who could be very pompous at times. The worst was an accountant who helped him balance his books.

On one visit to his father's shop, the accountant was particularly annoying. He said in an irritating voice, "You have your cash in the cash register, your debits in a cigar box, and your accounts receivable on a spindle. I don't see how you can run your business this way. How do you know what your profits are?"

The old fellow finally had had about enough from his boy so he took off his glasses (if you are a father and wear glasses, it's great because it buys you time) and said to his son, "Sit down." When his son started to protest, he simply motioned with his hand toward the chair and repeated more firmly, "Sit down."

Once his son was seated, the father looked at him, smiled slightly, and said, "Son, when I got off the boat from Italy I had only the pants I was wearing. Today your sister is an elementary school teacher, your brother is a doctor, and you're an accountant. I have a car, a house, and a good business. Everything is paid for. So, you add it all up and subtract the pants, and there's your profit!"

When we practice such simplicity we will be like people without guile or like little youngsters who are disarmingly honest. Instead of getting lost in complexity, we need to follow their example. Recalling a favorite story or interaction with the young is one of the fastest ways to accomplish this. Children can teach us clarity and simplicity when we interact with them. We need only watch them or listen to their stories to have this borne out. For instance, a friend related the following true story about two sisters widely separated in age.

The older sister (who was a freshman in college at the time) invited her younger sibling to spend the weekend with her at college. Toward the end of the weekend together, one of the older sister's roommates complimented the child in her sister's presence by saying, "She's the most precocious child I've ever met."

The older sister looked at her younger sister and said, "You don't know what that means, do you?"

"Yes I do," the younger sister replied. "It means I do and say things you don't expect me to do at my age."

Quite taken aback, the older sister asked, "Well, how ever did you know that?"

And the child replied quite simply, "Because I'm precocious!"

André Gide, the French dramatist, diarist, and novelist, once said, "I am erecting a barrier of simplicity between myself and the world." This is a goal all of us should consider seeking through a spirit of asceticism, gratefulness, and honesty—three very counter-cultural approaches in a world which prizes consumption, entitlement, and hype.

Asceticism and Gratefulness

The Greek philosopher and exponent of asceticism Diogenes felt that people had been given an easy life but spoiled it by "seeking after honey, cheese cakes, and unguents."[9] Some seven hundred years later, a spiritual thinker of early Christianity, John Chrysostom, would echo this theme:

A person who owns nothing—or, more precisely, who desires to own nothing, and regards nothing as a personal possession—in spirit owns everything. He can look at a beautiful valley, regardless of who the legal owner is, and rejoice in its beauty.[10]

Closer to our own time, Henry David Thoreau would present the value and fruit of simplicity in a slightly different way: "a [person] is rich in proportion to the things he can afford to let alone."[11]

Asceticism sounds very harsh and extreme, and I guess it can be. However, it depends on how we look at it, whether we practice it harshly. Kathleen Norris, in probably her most poetic and naturally spiritual book *Dakota,* rightly connects asceticism and gratitude: "The deprivation of Plains life [in the Dakotas] and monastic life tend to turn small gifts into treasures, and gratitude is one of the first flowers to spring forth when hope is rewarded and the desert blooms." She then goes on a few pages later to define asceticism as "a way of surrendering to reduced circumstances in a manner that enhances the whole person."

Clark Strand in his simple, helpful book *The Wooden Bowl* illustrates this in relating a story about his first teacher, an elderly Chinese hermit, Deh Chun, who lived out his final years in rural Tennessee:

> Being with Deh Chun was like dropping through a hole in everything that the world said was important—education, progress, money, sex, prestige. It was like discovering that nothing else mattered and all I needed was now—the moment—to survive. Sitting there in the little house, listening to the water boil, to the twigs crackling in the wood stove, I was temporarily removed from the game. That was the genius of his teaching, that he could bring forth that transformation without even saying a word.

> His was a state of complete simplicity. Like water, the direction of his life was downward, always seeking lower ground. When I met him he lived in a ramshackle two-room house heated by a wood stove the size of a typewriter. There was no furniture, only a few turned-over crates and several cardboard boxes in which he kept his clothes. His bed consisted of two sawhorses on top of which he had placed a three-foot by five-foot sheet of plywood and a piece of packing foam. I remember thinking

once that this bed suited him perfectly, his body was so light and small.

A similar structure in the other room served as a desk for writing letters and for painting his ink-wash Chinese landscapes. Propped against the back door were spades, a shovel, and a rake, tools he used to tend a plot of land the size of two king-size beds laid end to end. With the exception of tea, soybeans, peanut butter, molasses, and occasional wheat-flour, whatever he ate came from there.

He would talk about his garden, or more likely we would remain silent for a long while and then it would be time to leave.

Nowadays, in books on meditation, it has become standard practice to say that your teacher was a mirror that allowed you to see your true self. But that was not my experience with Deh Chun. It was more like floating weightless on the Dead Sea and looking up at an empty sky. There was a feeling of tremendous peace and freedom, but that was all. I didn't know anything after I was done. Trying to pin him down on some aspect of meditation was as pointless as trying to drive a stake through the air. He taught one thing and one thing only, and that he taught to perfection: meditation happens now.

After the first few visits to his house, I realized nothing pivotal was going to happen, but I kept returning anyway without knowing what it was about him that held my attention. I was a college student, and fairly typical of other nineteen-year-olds in that I was not particularly interested in spending time with someone four times my age. Especially someone, who by ordinary standards, was little better than a bum.

Long after his death, it is finally clear to me that he taught only by example. Recently, a friend of mine said of a certain Catholic priest, "He practices what he preaches, so he doesn't have to preach so loud." Deh Chun practiced so well he didn't have to preach at all.

Asceticism feeds simplicity. It helps us realize that love for others is not measured in quantity, but in the quality that marks the spirit of simplicity in true compassion. Often we feel it is in large lavish displays that we make the point we love someone. However, it is in the small, natural sharings of ourselves that we often (and usually unknowingly) make an impact. When I was in Cambodia I heard this story of an energetic missioner working in Central America:

I came into a little bit of money from some friends in the United States and I thought for a while about how best to spend it. Finally, the idea dawned on me that I would take the $200 and throw a party for children from the barrios.

So, I hired a bus and picked up the children and drove them off to a beautiful park they had never seen before because it was too far for them to walk.

When they got there I had a colorful tent set up for them. We had games to play, all kinds of food to eat including ice cream and candies of all shapes and flavors. What a day it was! Such great fun.

Then after we had driven them back to the barrio, I said goodbye to each child getting off the bus. But some of them hung around the bus for a few more moments before leaving and we talked a bit more as I could tell they and I didn't want the day to end.

During this time, I turned to a little smiling girl of eight and asked her what was the best thing she liked from the day. In response she looked up at me and said, "When you took my hand as we walked back to the bus."

Honesty

Honesty feeds simplicity. Simplicity is commonly understood as letting go of unnecessary external possessions. Beyond that, we have a greater need for simplicity within. *Sannyasis*—traveling holy persons in India—often carry only one *dhoti* to wear and have very few other personal possessions. This enables them to have the time and the room for more important activities of the spirit. They speak of spiritual simplicity, which means they must also travel light within themselves. Zen addresses this by saying that in becoming freer we don't obtain something, we drop it. Christian mystics refer to this as purity of heart. Psychologists and psychiatrists refer to it as to the need to be self-aware so we would have a less fractious inner self. We waste little energy on defenses and have more available for creativity and generativity.

In the end, they all speak of the naturalness and freedom we experience when we are totally honest with ourselves and know who we are; when we are simply ourselves and this becomes a gift to others who encounter us. True ordinariness is indeed tangible holiness. We know where the psychological furniture is within ourselves and we don't trip over it as often. The space within us that we share with others doesn't come from being totally empty of problems and immature behaviors. Instead it comes from humbly acknowledging that our whole lives consist of continual mistakes and encounters that can teach us. Knowing this can make all the difference.

Pema Chödrön, in her disarming book *When Things Fall Apart,* refers to this sense of persistent radical honesty as "groundlessness." By facing ourselves directly with a spirit of clarity and kindness and not seeking to hold on to anything but the pure unvarnished truth, a certain inner simplicity of spirit results. This will resist those things that would seduce our ego. Instead, everything, even the very unpleasant things in our lives will serve as teachers and free us even more.

Although she makes many good points in the book, it is the spirit of the message, her natural honesty, which compelled me to let go. Probably the most apt illustration of this is the way she tells the following story at the beginning of the book. In it I could actually *feel* "the wisdom of no escape" (the title of another of her books).

> We lived in northern New Mexico. I was standing in front of our adobe house drinking a cup of tea. I heard the car drive up and the door bang shut. Then he walked around the corner, and without warning he told me that he was having an affair and he wanted a divorce.
>
> I remember the sky and how huge it was. I remember the sound of the river and the steam rising up from my tea. There was no time, no thought, there was nothing—just the light and a profound, limitless stillness. Then I regrouped and picked up a stone and threw it at him.
>
> When anyone asks me how I got involved in Buddhism, I always say it was because I was so angry with my husband. The truth is that he saved my life. When that marriage fell apart, I tried hard—very, very hard—to go back to some kind of comfort, some kind of security, some kind of familiar resting place. Fortunately for me, I could never pull it off. Instinctively I knew

that annihilation of my old dependent, clinging self was the only way to go.

Chödrön and those of us who are blessed to be in the healing and helping professions recognize that this "annihilation" is actually a coming home to self. Maybe we are not there often or can't remember when last we felt relaxed within. Still, this is where most psychology and spirituality points—to be at home in your inner self, with yourself, others, and with God. The simplicity that encourages this requires that we travel light. The attitude that enhances this, at its very core, must include a renewed appreciation of *asceticism, gratefulness*, and *honesty*. One of the best places to discover this is in the practice of meditation.

Lesson 10

come
home
often

James Joyce wrote of a character in one of his novels, "Mr. Duffy lived a short distance from his body." This is often an apt description of most of us. Coming home to ourselves in the now is not easy. Not so much because we're afraid of being present to ourselves but because we have forgotten how to do it.

During the height of the famine in the Sudan, many people were displaced, including very little children. They wandered around in a daze seeking some food and drink. One little boy was so lost that, when asked, he couldn't even tell people his name, or worse yet, the village he came from—a special tragedy for Africans who are so identified with their tribe and village.

Spiritually and psychologically we are like this boy. Unlike him we can find our way home yet continue to wander aimlessly. We are not home for ourselves, others, or even God much of the time.

What a tragedy. We have received the gift of birth and the time to pass into adult life to gain wisdom, to share love, and to see God who is so present to us when we are at home in ourselves. But to be at home with ourselves requires the disciplines of solitude and silence.

Henri Nouwen saw solitude as the furnace of transformation. It was something sought by Jesus, by the fourth-century *abbas* and *ammas,* and through the ages by mystics, *sannyasis* (wandering holy persons), and by modern spiritual seekers of every stripe. A saying from desert *ammas* and *abbas* summed up this sentiment as follows: "Go and sit in your cell, and your cell will teach you everything."[12]

The goal could be the simple desire to quiet down and to let the dirt of the day settle. It might also be a wish to reflect and reorder one's priorities. Or it may possibly be something greater. As Anthony Storr points out in his book *Solitude*, the latter was the case with Admiral Byrd in undertaking his solo Antarctic expedition in the winter of 1934.

Aside from the meteorological . . . work, I had no important purposes. . . . Nothing whatsoever, except one man's desire to know that kind of experience to the full, to be by himself for a while and to taste peace and quiet and solitude long enough to find out how good they really are. . . . I wanted something more than privacy in the geographical sense. I wanted to sink roots into some replenishing philosophy.

Byrd's desires paid off. Despite nearly dying because of a faulty heater, he was nourished profoundly by the silence and solitude. It had a long-term effect on him, and he mused about this much later in his autobiography, *Alone.*

I did take away something that I had not fully possessed before: appreciation of the sheer beauty and miracle of being alive, and a humble set of values . . . civilization had not altered any ideas. I live more simply now, and with more peace.

Andrew Harvey echoes this sentiment in *A Journey in Ladakh.* In reflecting on the life led by the Buddhists who live in a very isolated section of India, he writes:

It is hard to survive the solitude of the winter and the lonely places . . . most of these people live simply and unsentimentally, they live with few needs, few prides, few vanities. They are tolerant to their old people, to their children, to each other.

As a result, Harvey sensed their peace and their ordinariness. They were people without guile and with a sense of natural respect. Their simplicity touched him deeply.

. . . when you see and feel this peace, this dignity, day after day in the most ordinary situations, in the way in which an old woman will make you tea, in the way she smiles at you from the fields, in the frankness of her answers.

I have felt the same sense of gentle awe and peace when I have been in rural communities, or places where cold, icy climates slow people down and leave them with an abundance of quiet, where they have time to relish a cup of strong tea and a thick piece of rich pie.

In my visits to Newfoundland I have found a rich sense of hospitality, a joy for life, and a good humor that makes life seem more real and certainly much simpler. An experience from there which I related in my book *Seeds of Sensitivity* I think is worth relating here again:

I have been to Newfoundland many times. But the first time I was there doing some consultant work, I particularly remember the flight back to Baltimore. I had just seated myself when a fellow dropped into the seat next to me, leaned over, and said to me: "Are you from Newfoundland? Are you a Newfee?" After I responded in the negative, he quickly followed with the question: "Well then, do you know where the Newfees keep their armies?" "No," I said. To this he replied: "Up their sleevies!" Making a face and laughing I said: "We're not going to do this for the whole flight are we?"

Then, a really chipper old fellow from one of the French areas of Newfoundland who was sitting three rows in front of us pulled down his fiddle from the overhead rack and started to sing and play. What a flight it was! What wonderful people Newfoundlanders are. I love them. Their joy and ability to poke fun at their own sense of simplicity made me more easily relax, accept my own ordinariness, and feel the sense of joy that was deep within me.

Even when I meet Newfoundlanders who have left "the rock" for other areas of Canada or the United States, they still retain their island traits. I have felt that same sense of retention with Christian monks or devout Buddhists. Even in a teeming city, they carry a sense of inner simplicity that bubbles over into generosity when you least expect it.

Once at a refugee center in Bangkok, a very childlike man who was blind in one eye wandered in. The Buddhist staff who took him in recognized all that he was up against. When I saw and asked about him, one of the staff thought for a moment, smiled, and said in English as he pointed to his own head, "Not full."

When I asked the director of the center, an American missionary, about the man, he said he had been with them for about six months. Then he added that when the man first arrived he had asked the staff what they could possibly do with someone with such emotional and intellectual challenges.

"What did they say?" I asked.

His face beamed. "They said, 'why love him, of course.'"

When feeling lost, overwhelmed, and looking for a direction that contains a beautiful spirit of love and simplicity like that of the Ladakhis, Newfoundlanders, or Thais, the natural question is: Where do I begin? The best answer is "start in the silence."

For instance, Zen roshi Shunryu Suzuki speaks of the value of silence in achieving simplicity. Suzuki ran a Zen center in San Francisco that attracted young college students who were trying to stop taking drugs. Many who came to the center moved from potentially destructive paths to ones filled with wonder and self-respect.

When asked how he did it, Suzuki replied, "Oh, I did nothing. I simply had them sit *zazen* and pretty soon they forgot about such things."[13]

But simply sitting silently in a group is not that easy. For when we sit in silence we create a vacuum in our consciousness. The preconscious rises into it to expose our lies and our games. Still, while Suzuki recognized the difficulty of facing the truths about ourselves that arise during meditation, he knew the deadly consequences of not doing it.

> When you are fooled by something else, the damage will not be so big. But when you are fooled by yourself, it is fatal. No more medicine.[14]

And so, coming home to yourself in quiet meditation, contemplation, reflection, prayer, or sitting *zazen* is not a luxury. But if you wish to live a simple, clear, full life, it is a necessity. Meditation is the food of life. Yet, to appreciate this and allow richly quiet periods to nourish life, several little steps must be taken.

Step One: Recognize Its Value

If we are to truly commit to a reflective, centered life, then we also need quiet periods of silence and solitude, even if it is only for ten minutes during a busy day. We must recognize how dangerous and aimless life can become if we don't take this time. No one is exempt. There is no spiritual graduation after which we are immune from falling prey to a life devoted to chasing the wrong things. Spiritual writer Henri Nouwen recognized this and put it quite eloquently in his journal published as *The Genesee Diary*:

> While teaching, lecturing, and writing about the importance of solitude, inner freedom, and peace of mind, I kept stumbling over my own

compulsions and illusions. What was driving me from one book to another, one place to another, one project to another? What made me think and talk about "the reality of the Unseen" with the seriousness of one who had seen all that is real? What was turning my vocation to be a witness to God's love into a tiring job? These questions kept intruding themselves into my few unfilled moments and challenging me to face my restless self. Maybe I spoke more about God than with him. Maybe my writing about prayer kept me from a prayerful life. Maybe I was more concerned about the praise of men and women than the love of God. Maybe I was slowly becoming a prisoner of people's expectations instead of a man liberated by divine promises. Maybe . . . it was not all that clear, but I realized that I would only know by stepping back and allowing the hard questions to touch me even if they hurt. But stepping back was not so easy. I had succeeded in surrounding myself with so many classes to prepare, lectures to give, articles to finish, people to meet, phone calls to make, and letters to answer, that I had come quite close to believing that I was indispensable.

When I took a closer look at this I realized that I was caught in a web of strange paradoxes. While complaining about too many demands, I felt uneasy when none were made. While speaking about the burden of letter writing, an empty mailbox made me sad. While fretting about tiring lecture tours, I felt disappointed when there were no invitations. While speaking nostalgically about an empty desk, I feared the day on which that would come true. In short: while desiring to be alone, I was frightened of being left alone. The more I became aware of these paradoxes, the more I started to see how much I had indeed fallen in love with my own compulsions and illusions, and how much I needed to step back and wonder, Is there a quiet stream underneath the fluctuating affirmations and rejections of my little world? Is there a still point where my life is anchored and from which I can reach out with hope and courage and confidence?

Step Two: Take Time Out Regularly

Time is a very precious gift. How we spend it, who we share it with, and whether we truly value it as a wondrous opportunity tells a lot about us and the way we live.

We take time for granted and even disrespect the very limited period we are given in our small life. As the Dalai Lama recognized in *The Path to Tranquility*:

Try to develop a deep conviction that the present human body has great potential and that you shall never waste even a single minute of its use.

Not taking any essence of this precious human existence, but just wasting it, is almost like taking poison while being fully aware of the consequences of doing so.

It is very wrong for people to feel deeply sad when they lose some money, yet when they waste the precious moments of their lives they do not have the slightest feeling of repentance.

Taking time out, whether in groups or alone, helps us come home to ourselves. Silence offers pristine aloneness. We can come to appreciate this space and then seek it out like cool water on a hot day or a cozy fire on a frigid night. We will seek to do it regularly. It's like meeting an old friend for breakfast, not out of duty or guilt, but rather for our own fulfillment.

Step Three: Honor Your Resistances

However, if a place for meditation were just a place of peace, more people would do it more often. But such a place is also a place of life, of truth, and therefore of challenge. So the quiet spaces we treasure in our fantasies will never become a reality in our schedule, unless we come to know and honor our resistances. In this way, when our resistances surface, they will not damage our silence but will be welcomed like old friends or restless children who need understanding, patience, and love.

Some of these old friends and restless children take the form of:

~ Worries about what we need to do or didn't do

~ Resentment of others

~ Shame about ourselves

~ Boredom and restlessness because we are always on the move

~ A stream of "great ideas" that we must write down now

~ Regrets about how we have lived

~ Fears about living differently because, after all, what will people think? How will they react?

~ Concern about how hard change will be

~ Discouragement that our prayer or meditation doesn't seem as good, refreshing, or as natural as that of those who teach or write about it

~ Feelings that meditation is a luxury, lacks importance, or isn't as practical or as effective as action

Because no one warns us about these natural resistances, many people are discouraged at the very onset of a life nourished by quiet prayer. This is a shame, and it is also unnecessary.

The reality is that *everyone* has an imperfect prayer life. For as long as you meditate, you will be a beginner. There is no spiritual graduation. We must walk through the chaff if we are to appreciate the wheat in our lives. Toward the end of his life, while finally living as a hermit, Thomas Merton wrote this question in his diary, "Am I so full of nonsense that [solitude] will cast me out?"

In silence and solitude, we clear our consciousness and create a vacuum. Since nature abhors vacuums, the thoughts, impulses, memories, and other unpleasant material in our preconsciousness rise to fill it. Sometimes this information has been consciously suppressed or unconsciously repressed because we didn't want to face it.

However, avoiding it only makes us live a life that is so much less than it could be. Therein is the substance of the lies, the games, and the dark realities of our inner life. As author James Baldwin once said, "People cling to their hate so stubbornly . . . because once hate is gone, they will be forced to deal with their own pain."

In silence and solitude, we face our own mortality and our utter aloneness. Rather than only seeing Henri Nouwen's inner stream of refreshment as a metaphor for the inner life, we find our own desert.

In his book *Sahara Unveiled*, William Langewiesche writes that in the physical desert it is "so lonely that migrating birds land beside people just for the company." Such an image helps reveal the feeling experienced in our inner desert. Loneliness is a part of life. We are born alone and die alone. Our fears, angers, sorrows, and hurts are all our own. No matter how well someone knows or loves us, he or she will never see us or the world through our eyes. In *A Vow of Conversation*, Merton offers insightful words: "one must struggle in loneliness . . . but why desperation? This is not necessary."

Meditation also joins us with others in the world who are seeking to live in the now with purity, self-awareness, peace, joy, and unselfconsciousness. Meditation fosters unitive experiences in which we can feel one with nature, life, the world.

At the very least, silence and solitude lead us to see the big lie in our compulsive lives: We think we will have more time, better health, more fulfilling work, closer friends, later. If we buy this great falsehood, then surely we will merely exist until we do die—probably in the midst of planning or preparing for the future.

Know the Benefits

So, the challenge before us is to go within. We need to do this not so we become more preoccupied with ourselves but for discovery. As Rainer Maria Rilke admonishes in his work *Letters to a Young Poet*:

> You are looking outward, and that above all you should not do. Nobody can counsel and help you, nobody. There is only one single way. Go into yourself.

If your daily life seems poor, do not blame it; blame yourself, tell yourself that you are not poet enough to call forth its riches; for to the creator there is no poverty and no poor indifferent place . . . you [also] . . . have your childhood, that precious, kingly possession, that treasure house of memories. . . . Turn your attention thither. Try to cause the submerged sensation of that ample past; your personality will grow more firm, your solitude will widen and will become a dusty dwelling past which the noise of others goes by far away.

Solitude, when joined with silence and a meditative spirit, will produce other benefits as well:

~ A decrease in driven, grasping, and other compulsive behaviors
~ An opportunity to refocus and let the day settle down (When Thomas Merton found that the day's activities and his thoughts about them led to confusion and regret, he would sit quietly, drink some tea, and read a psalm. This quiet reflective rhythm would correct his perspective and let things take the proper place in his life.)
~ A chance to laugh at ourselves
~ A chance to be more gentle and friendlier with ourselves
~ An opening to new space and freedom within because our self-imposed demands and expectations of others no longer have a psychological chokehold on us

~ A new vision of how each day—even apparently tough ones—can become invigorating for us.

Sogyal Rinpoche in *The Tibetan Book of Living and Dying* puts it this way:

> The gift of learning to meditate is the greatest gift you can give yourself in this life. For it is only through meditation that you can understand the journey to discover your true nature, and so find the stability and confidence you will need to live, and die, well. Meditation is the road to enlightenment. . . .

> Our lives are lived in intense and anxious struggle, in a swirl of speed and aggression, in competing, grasping, possessing, and achieving, forever burdening ourselves with extraneous activities and preoccupations. Meditation is the exact opposite.

There is also a new gratefulness that comes with a life of prayer and reflection. A number of years ago my daughter lived in Florida and we had an interaction which confirmed this relationship between appreciation for life and being a person of prayer. I shared it in the book *Everyday Simplicity* and offer it again here:

> I love to visit South Florida and for the past few years I have had an additional reason to visit more often—my daughter Michaele lives and works there. On one visit I commented on the

remarkable colors of the evening sky. Privately, I wondered if people there ever got used to the display. Michaele smiled and nodded. Then, after a few seconds, she said in almost a whisper while smiling gently, "Every time I look up at the sky here in Florida, I feel like I am on a vacation with God."

As I was to later realize, this seemingly off-handed poignant comment did not come easily. It was the product of practicing a constant "discipline of gratefulness." Michaele eventually shared with me that on a number of occasions she actually felt quite lost and abandoned by God. Yet in retrospect she could see and appreciate that "God was telling me something and I wasn't listening, giving me something and I wasn't receiving."

Later, when we spoke again about the beautiful Florida evenings, she honed her spirituality of gratefulness even further for me. She said, "I know the sunsets are for everyone. But as in observing other works of art, what each of us receives from them are personal gifts from God. They are uniquely ours."

Practicing reflection and/or prayer requires no special equipment or extraordinary place. It is simply a matter of attitude.

Step Four: Have a Simple Practice

How we meditate is up to each of us. We must take off our shoes and meet life in our own way. However, the following basic ideas which most of us were taught at some time or another are worth repeating here:

1. Find a quiet place, alone if possible.

2. Sit up straight.

3. Close your eyes or keep them slightly open looking a few feet in front of you.

4. Count slow, naturally exhaled breaths from one to four and repeat the process.

5. Relax and let stray thoughts move through you like a slow-moving train, repeating themes; observe them objectively, then let them go.

6. Experience living in the now.

For those who are religious and seek a personal relationship with God, the following variation is offered:

1. Find a quiet place to sit and relax.

2. Put yourself in the presence of a loving God and wrap yourself in gratitude. If you don't have these feelings, pray for them as you continue.

3. Take either a centering word (e.g. Jesus) or read a few passages from the Bible or a spiritual book.

4. Sit with the spirit of what you have read or quietly repeat the centering word over and over again. If you become aware of anything else or are distracted, just let the issue move through your mind and out. If it persists, then hand it over to God rather than preoccupying yourself with it, which, after all, serves no purpose.

5. Sit quietly and lovingly like this with the Lord for ten or twenty minutes a day on a regular basis and your relationship with God will grow.

The Joy and Peace of Coming Home

Coming home to ourselves in prayer, meditation, or sitting *zazen* brings much more than wisdom. It helps us soften life's tempo, encourages us to be understanding of and friendlier with ourselves, helps us to see and accept the simplicity of life, and tempers our arrogance. Our ambitions, schedules, expectations, worries, plans, and anxieties don't seem to have such a grasp on us. In a mysterious way they become less pressing. We become a little less uncomfortable with ourselves. We want to live more fully and simply and are not put off from this by the complaints, fears, and spirit of entitlement to which so many in the world seem to fall prey.

We start to finally understand, maybe for the first time, what the author Henry James meant when he wrote,

Live all you can
it's a mistake not to.
It doesn't so much matter
what you do in particular,
So long as you have had your life.
If you haven't had that
What have you had?[15]

Epilogue

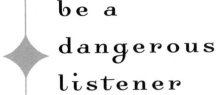

be a dangerous listener

uthor Karl Shapiro said of noted American poet and critic Randall Jarrell that he was "a great, you might say, a *dangerous* listener."[16]

In *The Book of Tibetan Elders*, Sandy Johnson beautifully explores a spiritual land of wisdom and compassion where sages come from a long lineage of people passionate about the search for inner peace.

> Shambala is a beautiful city where extraordinary beings live cut off from the outside world by their own volition. It is a place of peace.

> . . . Some Tibetans even view Shambala as a metaphor for one's own inner spiritual journey

and dedicate their lives to finding it within themselves.

One way to take a journey to our own "Shambala" is to learn to listen deeply, maybe dangerously, to our inner self. It will lead to change and to life.

As Phil Cousineau, in his book *The Art of Pilgrimage,* rightly recognizes, "Listening closely is nearly a lost art, but a retrievable one. The soul thrives on it. . . . Words heard by chance have been known to change lives. . . . Listen as though your life depends on it. It does."[17] Listening closely, listening dangerously, listening as though our lives depend on it, means listening from the heart.

When we seek to listen from the heart we recognize that we are not free in so many, many ways in our lives. In his classic work *Beginning to Pray,* Anthony Bloom writes:

> There is a passage in Dickens' *Pickwick Papers* which is a very good description of my life and probably also of your lives. Pickwick goes to the club. He hires a cab and on the way he asks innumerable questions. Among the questions, he says, "Tell me, how is it possible that such a mean and miserable horse can drive such a big and heavy cab?" The cabbie replies, "It's not a question of the horse, Sir, it's a question of the wheels," and Mr. Pickwick says, "What do you mean?" The cabbie answers, "You see, we have a magnificent pair of wheels which are so well

oiled that it is enough for the horse to stir a little for the wheels to begin to turn and then the poor horse must run for its life." Take the way in which we live most of time. We are not the horse that pulls, we are the horse that runs away from the cab in fear of its life.

In order to avoid being pushed by our attachments, we need to listen for and hear the emotional noise when we are upset. Sensing unpleasant feelings such as anger, anxiety, or great stress helps us grasp areas where freedom is lacking in our lives.

In addition, how we listen to or experience life helps us recognize that most often it is life's ordinary—not extraordinary—elements that contain holiness and peace. The following simple reminiscence by a former student, who was interested in the integration of spirituality and psychology, illustrates this beautifully.

> When I was a child I spent many holidays on my uncle and aunt's small farm. One special memory is of the time spent in their cowshed.
>
> In the evenings as they milked the cows, I would sit on a little stool, surrounded by kittens and dogs, and as they milked their cows they often would pray. Maybe a rosary or prayers for the neighbors, a good crop. Prayer was natural, linked to the rhythm of their milking. Amidst the very earthy sounds, smells, and sights of an ordinary cowshed, I sensed the presence of God.

When they were finished it was my task to run my fingers over the top of the milk pail, gathering some froth, and bless each cow with the sign of the cross. My aunt would speak to me of the importance of caring and being grateful for these creatures of God.

Then, on returning to their house, we would have supper, and often this would mean fried homemade bread and rashers. The smell of bacon frying to this day is like incense for me, evoking and reminding me of the presence of God.

How we listen to our lives determines whether we simply categorize things as bad or good, whether we spend our lives running toward or away from certain people or interactions, or if we greet the possibilities in all of life.

A number of years ago a wise and holy person came to visit with me. A true spiritual master, she had guided many people in their search for God. She was seeing me because of the sudden occurrence of panic attacks.

On her second visit, we were walking around the lake near my office. It was early spring so the light green leaves and pink-white dogwood petals topped the trees like a delicate lace. It was so calming, even she seemed to absorb some of its peace.

As we completed about half the walk, she looked at me with concern and asked, "Will I get over these panic attacks?"

To which I responded: "Oh, without a doubt. This shouldn't take long at all. However, because of this, I have a spiritual concern."

Upon hearing this, her expression showed both relief and surprise, so I explained, "The panic attacks have shaken you out of your habitual ways of living. You no longer see yourself and your life as you did prior to the attacks. So, although they are unpleasant, they've given you a chance to look at everything anew. The ironic spiritual problem for us is whether we can make the most of this time before the panic completely disappears again."

Any occurrence that moves us out of taking life for granted is a gift. Dramatic things do this. So, adolescence, male and female menopause, even trauma, bring possibility with the pain. The question is whether we will listen to and take advantage of these periods of imbalance. Few people do. Just look around. If all suffering led to wisdom and insight without any effort or strength, we would be surrounded by a sea of saints.

There needs to be a sense of faithfulness to the spiritual journey no matter what we are facing. As the Tibetan teacher Chogyam Trungpa admonished, "If you have begun [the journey within], it is best to finish." Wisdom and faithfulness help in this regard.

Riding Our Inner Dragons

In Paulo Coelho's novel *The Alchemist*, one of the characters speaks of the desert as we speak of the journey within:

"Once you get into the desert, there's no going back," said the camel driver. "And when you can't go back, you have to worry only about moving forward. The rest is up to Allah, including the danger."

The same can be said of compassion. Sister Helen Prejean, the author of the book *Dead Man Walking*, told me and others when we were lecturing in a program together, "If you are going to do something for the poor, the abused, or the imprisoned, above all, be faithful. People with broken lives often come from lives with broken promises."

Together the journeys of inner wisdom and compassion that have been encouraged in *Riding the Dragon* are actually the key elements of a faith-full journey or *pilgrimage*. In a pilgrimage, we don't just drift or rush through life. Instead, it is a way to prove our faith and find answers to our deepest questions. The difference between pilgrim and tourist is the intention of attention, the quality of listening.

One of the main points emphasized and re-emphasized in this book is that a fulfilled life demands we proceed on the spiritual journey. Like a true pilgrimage, it is an arduous, intentional one not to be taken naively, without forethought and serious motivation. A pilgrimage involving the search to be wise and compassionate does involve hard choices, brave decisions, and bold ideas. That is how we discover and strengthen our inner self so that we may be good-hearted with others.

And so, this inner pilgrimage, just like an actual sacred geographical journey, is, in the words of Phil Cousineau, nothing less than a "way to prove your faith and find answers to your deepest questions."[18] So, it is no surprise, then, that the traditional farewell among the people of Egypt and many of the Arabic world for those leaving on a journey to a sacred destination is:

Be Safe and Well

Peace, Love, Courage.

I echo the same blessing for you. You have listened dangerously; you have listened from the heart. You have absorbed, and sought to apply these dragon-riding lessons, and now depart to continue on an inner pilgrimage through the deserts and oases of your own life.

Some Readings
I Have Found
Helpful

Inner Journeys:
Autobiographical Fragments

There are periods in people's lives when exploration of their inner self parallels the changes occurring in their daily public lives as well. Some contemporary classics that fit into this category are: Anne Lamott's *Traveling Mercies: Some Thoughts on Faith* (Pantheon, 1999); Kathleen Norris's *Dakota: A Spiritual Geography* (Ticknor and Fields, 1993); Mitch Albom's *Tuesdays with Morrie: An Old Man, A Young Man, and Life's Greatest Lessons* (Doubleday, 1997); Annie Dillard's *The Writing Life* (Harper Collins, 1989); George Crane's *Bones of the Master: A Buddhist Monk's Search for the Lost Heart of China* (Doubleday, 2000); Andrew Harvey's *Journey in Ladakh* (Houghton Mifflin, 1984); Peter Matthiessen's *Nine-Headed Dragon River* (Shambhala, 1985); Rainer Maria Rilke's *Letters to a Young Poet* (Norton, 1954); Doris Grumbach's *Fifty Days of Solitude*

(Beacon, 1994); Richard Bode's *First You Have to Row a Little Boat* (Warner, 1993); Sandy Johnson's *The Book of Tibetan Elders: The Life Stories and Wisdom of the Great Spiritual Masters of Tibet* (Riverhead, 1999); and Henri Nouwen's *Genesee Diary: Report from a Trappist Monastery* (Doubleday, 1976).

Contemporary Biographies/Autobiographies:

Relaxing with a well-written biography or autobiography of a fascinating person of substance is one of my favorite joys. Their lives stir me to respect the grandeur of my own so I can risk living it fully with a sense of care, compassion, gratitude, and commitment. Each excellent biography should not keep us at a distance from the person about whom we are reading; rather it should call us to live rather than observe life.

Contemporary biographies that have done this for me include: Michael Mott's *The Seven Mountains of Thomas Merton* (Houghton Mifflin, 1984); Robert Coles' *Dorothy Day: A Radical Devotion* (Perseus, 1987); David Chadwick's *Crooked Cucumber: The Life and Zen Teachings of Shunryu Suzuki* (Broadway, 1999); Janet Wallach's *Desert Queen: The Extraordinary Life of Gertrude Bell—Adventurer, Advisor to Kings, Ally of Lawrence of Arabia* (Doubleday, 1996); Dalai Lama's *Freedom in Exile*

(Harper, 1991); and Shirley du Boulay's *Beyond the Darkness: A Biography of Bede Griffiths* (Doubleday, 1998).

Quotes From the Masters

Powerful wisdom in short doses has quite an impact if we read and absorb quotes from people we admire. Abraham Heschel's *I Asked for Wonder* (edited by Samuel Dresner, Crossroad, 1983) and His Holiness The Dalai Lama's *The Path to Tranquility* (edited by Renuka Singh, Viking, 1999) are but two examples of compilations of selections from the writings of a well-known spiritual figure. Of course, there are many other collections from single authors or ones that contain quotes from an array of sources. One of the more creative examples of a book of quotes from more than one tradition is Anthony de Mello's *One Minute Wisdom* (Doubleday, 1986). It is a series of edited and paraphrased dialogues between a master and disciple drawn from the traditional folklore and stories of the major world religions. It is truly a delight.

Wisdom From the East

I have been deeply affected in the past ten years with recent books on American and Tibetan Buddhism and Zen. The most helpful of these titles were: David Brazier's *Zen Therapy* (Wiley, 1997);

Pema Chödrön's *When Things Fall Apart: Transcending the Sorrows of the Human Mind* (Shambhala, 1997); Jack Kornfield's *After the Ecstasy, The Laundry* (Doubleday, 2000) and *A Path with Heart* (Doubleday, 1993); Sogyal Rinpoche's *The Tibetan Book of Living and Dying* (Harper, 1992); David Schuller's *The Little Zen Companion* (Workman, 1994); Ram Dass's *Journey of Awakening* (Bantam, 1978); Thomas Merton's *The Way of Chuang Tzu* (New Directions, 1965); and Jon Kabat-Zinn's *Wherever You Go, There You Are* (Hyperion, 1994).

These books have a wealth of information on such essential topics as:

- ~ Impermanence
- ~ Letting go
- ~ Meditation
- ~ Inner longing
- ~ Attachment
- ~ Facing death
- ~ The "gates of awakening"
- ~ Emptiness
- ~ Solitude and silence
- ~ The spiritual life
- ~ The burden of being judgmental
- ~ Wisdom and compassion

If you've never read books on eastern wisdom and daily life, the ones listed above would be a great start.

Desert Wisdom

These introductions to the spirituality and sayings of the Desert Fathers and Mothers of the fourth and fifth centuries are: Thomas Merton's *The Wisdom of the Desert* (New Directions, 1960); Henri Nouwen's *The Way of the Heart* (HarperCollins, 1981) and Yushi Nomura's *Desert Wisdom*. Three chapters on this topic you might enjoy as well are contained in Kenneth Leech's *Experiencing God* (Harper Collins, 1985); Robert Wicks' *Touching the Holy* (Ave Maria Press, 1992); and Peter France's *Hermits* (St. Martin's Press, 1996).

Some other popular books which deal with desert wisdom are: Belden Lane's *The Solace of Fierce Landscapes* (Oxford University Press, 1998); Anselm Gruen's *Heaven Begins Within You* (Crossroad, 1999); Andrew Louth's *The Wilderness of God* (Abingdon, 1991); and Gregory Mayer's *Listen to the Desert* (Triumph, 1996).

For a more scholarly treatment of the subject, I would suggest Benedicta Ward's three books *The Sayings of the Desert Fathers* (Cistercian, 1975), *Harlots of the Desert* (Cistercian, 1987), and *The Wisdom of the Desert Fathers* (SLG, 1975). She also wrote a wonderful introduction to *The Lives of the Desert Fathers*, translated by Norman Russell (Cistercian, 1980). Other serious works include: Helen Waddell's *The Desert Fathers* (Ann Arbor, 1957); Columba Stewart's *The World of the Desert*

Fathers (SLG, 1986); and Douglas Burton-Christie's *The Word in the Desert* (Oxford University Press, 1993).

Some Additional "Gems"

Other worthwhile books that have had an impact on my life and work are: Viktor Frankl's *Man's Search for Meaning* (Washington Square Press, 1959); David Burns' *Feeling Good* (Signet, 1980); Joseph Ciarrocchi's *Why Are You Worrying?* (Paulist, 1995); Judith Herman's *Trauma and Recovery* (Basic Books, 1992); Anthony Storr's *Solitude* (Ballantine, 1988); and Phil Cousineau's *The Art of Pilgrimage* (Conari Press, 1998).

notes

1. Shunryu Suzuki quoted in David Chadwick's wonderful biography, *The Crooked Cucumber* (New York: Broadway Books, 1999).

2. Margaret Mitchell, source unknown.

3. Frank O'Connor quoted in Robert J. Wicks, *Self-Ministry Through Self-Understanding.* Chicago: Loyola University Press, 1983, p. 98

4. Dorothy Day, source unknown.

5. William Hulme. *Managing Ministry.* San Francisco: Harper and Row, 1985, pp. 54-55.

6. Constance FitzGerald, "Impasse and the Dark Night of the Soul," in *Living with the Apocalypse*, Tilden Edwards, ed., New York: Harper and Row, 1984.

7. Abba Macarius was one of the desert fathers of the fourth century. See Thomas Merton, *The Wisdom of the Desert* (New York: New Direction, 1960) for more quotes.

8. A version of this famous story appears in *Mother Teresa* (edited by Becky Benate and Joseph Durepos). Novato, California: New World Library, 1989, pp. 39-40.

9. Diogenes quoted in a wonderful book by Peter France, *Hermits: The Insights of Solitude* (New York: St. Martin's Press, 1997).

10. John Chrysostom, *On Living Simply* (compiled by Robert Van de Weyer). Ligouri, Missouri: Triumph, 1996, p. 37.

11. Henry David Thoreau, quoted in *Pearls of Wisdom* (compiled by Jerome Angel and Walter Glange). New York: Harper & Row, 1988, p. 49.

12. *Desert Wisdom* (translated and art by Yushi Nomura). Maryknoll, New York: Orbis, 2001, p. 14.

13. Shunryu Suzuki, quoted in *The Crooked Cucumber*, p. 308.

14. *Ibid.,* p. 111.

15. Henry James, quoted in *Pearls of Wisdom*, p. 43.

16. Randall Jarrell quoted in Richard Kehl, *Silver Departures.* La Jolla, California: The Green Tiger Press, 1983, p. 25.

17. Phil Cousineau, *The Art of Pilgrimage.* Berkeley, California: Conari Press, 1998, p. 39.

18. *Ibid.*, p. xvii.

DR. ROBERT WICKS has been helping people "take a measure of their lives" for more than 30 years now, always working from the perspective that "difficult times can offer graced moments in a more striking ways than the good times can." The author of more than twelve books on spirituality and personal growth, he is a professor in the Graduate Programs in Pastoral Counseling at Loyola College in Maryland, the largest program of its type in the world. Dr. Wicks, who received his doctorate in psychology from Hahnemann Medical College, is a graduate of both Fairfield and St. John's Universities. He has also taught in universities and professional schools of psychology, medicine, social work, theology, and nursing, including Bryn Mawr's Graduate School of Social Work and Social Research, Princeton Theological Seminary, and Stritch School of Medicine in Chicago.

Wicks maintains a private practice and specializes in the prevention of secondary stress (the pressure that results from reaching out to others in need) and the integration of psychology and spirituality. He is a frequent lecturer in the United States, Canada, India, Europe, Central America, Asia, and New Zealand.

He has worked with professionals from the English-speaking international community in Cambodia helping the Khmer people rebuild their nation following years of terror and torture; and was also responsible for the psychological debriefing of relief workers evacuated from Rwanda during its bloody civil war.